Look For
the
Silver Lining

Stephen Lockwood

Published by

MELROSE BOOKS

An Imprint of Melrose Press Limited
St Thomas Place, Ely
Cambridgeshire
CB7 4GG, UK
www.melrosebooks.com

FIRST EDITION

The Author asserts his moral right to
be identified as the author of this work

Cover designed by Bryan Carpenter

ISBN 1 905226 55 1

Printed and bound in Great Britain by:
CPI Antony Rowe, Bumpers Farm,
Chippenham, Wiltshire, SN14 6LH, UK

Disclaimer

Many of the names of persons portrayed in this book have been changed to protect their individual identities.

Foreword

Making the decision to move on in life when you know some aspect of it has reached its sell-by date requires great courage. We all fear change and the unknown, but there is nothing more frustrating than watching someone who is stuck in a destructive rut, dithering about, unable to make a clean break. People in this situation find all the excuses under the sun to override everything their hearts, brains and instincts are telling them, clinging on to the safety of the familiar.

Quite often this can be at the cost of undermining their own health. Ironically, the more successful people are, the harder it can be for them to face the need for change in some major aspect of their lives. The fight for control and power will only fill us with fear. Fear, in turn, fills us with negative thoughts.

This book may not provide sufficient stimulus for the intellectual reader.

Mine is not a story of physical pain, but emotional pain; injuries that no one can see, but are a very severe handicap, with a very long healing process. Had I been born fifty years later, I may not have felt the embarrassment and humiliation from the stigma that came from an illegitimate childhood, which I found difficult to accept into my adult years. Now, as children are being born out of wedlock from all areas of society, that social stigma has been somewhat diluted, though this for many can cause untold social and domestic problems in later life, whilst breaking down the family unit.

Acknowledgements

My thanks go to my dear Mum who without sharing my life through triumphs and adversities I could not have produced this book.

My thanks go to my dear son Dale for his love and affection he has shown through both difficult and happy times.

My thanks also go to Mum and sister Sandra who have patiently endured the past months since I revealed to them this publication.

My thanks go to my friends Tony and Mary, and to my present employers who have all shared my secret in confidence over many years.

My thanks go to my friends Rita and Gordon, Judith and Neil, and Jan for simply just being there.

My heartfelt thanks go to Helen for being a special part of my life, and for her actions early in 1995 which allowed me to continue my life and move forward.

Although thank you does not seem enough, I would like to express my deepest thanks to Austin and his team at Melrose Books for their dedication and hard work which has gone into publishing this book and making my dream come true.

My thanks go to Judy, my secretary, who has provided an excellent professional service in typing up my manuscript.

Finally, my thanks go to all the Fell Runners who I had the pleasure of running alongside over many years in the Lake District and the Yorkshire Dales, and who unwittingly had played a part in keeping me strong as we shared so many happy times, leaving me with memories to treasure.

Introduction

I have to write this now, Christmas Eve. The thought of writing a book has been lying dormant in my mind for ten years or more, but could never have been practised until now because I have always been so full of life physically, which brings me to why I have to write it now. I just cannot stand physically or mentally one more moment of not doing anything.

I opened my shop, cosy and welcoming with natural fragrances of dried flowers and the sound of traditional Christmas carols, at 9.00 a.m. on Thursday, 24th December, 1992. Thursday is Market Day in Hebden Bridge, West Yorkshire, which can be a quiet day in the shop. The beginning of the week was an unexpected bonus, as I don't normally open on Mondays. However, my in-laws were visiting us from London, to stay over the festive season, and had offered to open the shop for me. The takings that day were a pleasant surprise. I had expected the week to get steadily busier leading up to Christmas Eve; however, it got steadily worse. Having used up all my materials for making flower arrangements, which is what my business is, the shop was swept clean and every attention paid to detail ready for my Christmas Eve shoppers.

By 1.00 p.m. I had not had one person in the shop. I was desperately frustrated, to the point where I put down my "Pennine" magazine, which I had read from front to back in an attempt to alleviate my boredom – it didn't work – and picked up a pen and what happened to be a full-page note pad. I started to write furiously and naturally at a speed I had never written before. It was as though I was taking my first breath of air as a "new born". Ten months now of spasmodic customer-controlled work in a new business and I felt as if I had been drowning. Closed shop 4.45 p.m. Total customers, four.

Continued Wednesday, 30th December, 1992

I woke at 6.00 a.m. to the weak, whining sound of Jack trying his best to alert me that he was about to have an accident. Jack is our nine and a half year old Rottweiler who, over the last six months, has been rapidly losing the use of his back legs, and is now becoming incontinent.

As I fumbled for the door keys and made my way to the landing where Jack sleeps, I was relieved, after putting the light on, to find I had reached him in time. Quickly unlocking the door, I ushered him outside, trying not to think of the sudden change in temperature for him, as his sympathetic eyes looked up at me under his wrinkled brow. No greying, his face has still got the definite rich black and tan markings, so distinctive and characteristic of his breed, as when he was a pup. 'Come on! Come on!' I whispered, as I slowly walked him down the garden.

I braced myself in the thin air, knowing we had just had three weeks of very hard frost; the temperature must again be minus. Pulling my dressing gown together I ran back indoors. My wife, Helen, was still submerged under the warm flannelette sheets. I desperately needed another hour in bed if I was to survive till next Christmas in that shop, so I jumped back in beside her and settled down.

The alarm clock rang at 7.30 a.m. I hadn't got back into a deep sleep, so getting up for the second time wasn't too bad. On pulling back the curtains I could see what looked like snow but was in fact a very heavy frost on the tops of the valley, confirming my suspicion of the temperature earlier when in the garden.

We had only our two selves to get ready for work this morning, as our five-year old son, Dale, was with his grandparents at their second home in Barkisland, which is in the next valley to where we live.

Whilst Helen busied herself ready for work, I fed Jack. We were both due in Hebden Bridge for work at 9.00 a.m. Fortunately, the car wasn't frozen up, which was the first time in about three weeks. We live on the valley side and somehow seemed to miss the frost this morning. Being a thrifty couple, we make an effort to travel to work in one vehicle now we both work in Hebden Bridge. I dropped Helen off at the pharmacy, where she works as a technician, and walked round to the shop.

My shop is up off ground level, on the first floor of a three hundred year old stone mill, now converted into shops and business premises. A large branch of holly, which I forgot to take inside, still hung over the door with its £1.50 price tag on, its berries beginning to shrivel – I knew I wouldn't get my £1.50 now.

As I opened the door and walked in, I was greeted with the familiar natural sweet smell of herbs and dried flowers, which I had maintained whilst stocking the shop over the last ten months. Before putting the lights on, I had to take a few moments to myself. Two thoughts were occupying my mind. Firstly, I was so relieved to find everything as I had left it on Christmas Eve, as my wife had told me of numerous shops that had been vandalised over the years in the town. Secondly, and most importantly, was "spring". As I was stocking the shop for Christmas in October, although I enjoyed it, I was very cautious, knowing that Christmas is relatively short in comparison to the rest of the year. All I could think of was to be able to sell sufficient stock to purchase new supplies for spring. I had to tell myself I should be grateful that, although Christmas Eve was so quiet, I had sold most of the stock in the previous eight weeks.

Well, on with the lights. I had heard from other shopkeepers in the town that there could be quite a few people around in the week between Christmas and New

Year: though I wasn't going to build up on this, as I was still suffering from last week's anticlimax.

Though there was little to prepare for opening, I was able to cope with the fact that here I was again, all day, with possibly no customers and literally nothing to do, because I had come alive again on Christmas Eve by starting to write this book which, after half a dozen pages, I had to leave.

It is now 5.00 p.m. and has been a better day. Twelve customers in all, some of whom actually spent, plus my wife, who always tries to call in at least once to reassure me, when I'm at my lowest, that there is nothing wrong with my product, but there is a recession on and I am up one flight of stairs.

So, an improvement on last week, but it is my newfound occupation, my writing, which has kept me sane! This I must try to keep a close secret until completed, so I must bring this introduction to a close before my wife comes to collect me to go shopping. I am not very far into this book but already can feel something that is very familiar to me, the flow of adrenalin. This I find very strange because I am obviously sitting down whilst writing and have always associated adrenalin with something more active. As mentioned earlier, I have always been used to physical work and leisure.

What will transpire from this writing I really do not know. I would very much like it to be published, not because I want or am trying to be a writer, but because I would dearly love this to be read by someone who may have a similar standing in life as myself and, therefore, may find it of some help by way of inspiration. I have picked up my pen with such a force within me to write, and now find it difficult to stop; I don't want to stop, so I hope you will stay with me as I continue to write this book in my own words.

Chapter One

Someone once told me that people become who they are by the way their parents mould them from an early age, either intentionally or as a matter of course through the effect their parents have on them whilst growing up. I'm not sure if this is totally true. However, for whatever element of truth there is in it, I am my mother's son. Hopefully, you will have judged for yourself by the end of this book how much effect my mother has had on me throughout my life.

Born on 23rd February, 1929 to a working-class family, my mother, Laura Clemence, was the youngest of three daughters. My grandparents were later to have a son. My grandfather had always wanted a boy, my mother told me. Sadly, due to food poisoning from tinned crab, my mother and her younger brother were rushed into hospital, where baby Walter, named after my grandfather, later died. Mum suffered from severe convulsions, but survived.

Mum Aged 17, 1946 in Luddenden Valley.

Mum third from left on front row in dark dress next to teacher. School photograph 1939 (ten years old).

Now there were three girls. They say there is an odd one out in three; two is a couple and three a crowd and all that. Mum says she was the odd one out. Whilst growing up, one of my aunties told me mum got more attention from my grandparents than they did; maybe due to her illness. Consequently, this made things more difficult for mum's relationship with her two sisters.

As the years went by, mum seemed to rebel against all the ideas and everyday suggestions her two older sisters had for her. Out of the two, the elder, my Auntie Margaret, seemed to have the softer nature and apparently was kept from associating too much with mum by the middle sister, Auntie Rita.

Their home was a small farmstead in the Luddenden Valley on the Pennines of West Yorkshire. Over the years I have listened to the stories mum has told me of their meagre way of life compared to today's standards. Everyday chores: black-leading the fireplace, scrubbing stone-flagged floors, carrying water for household chores from the well across the road, which filled from the moors' natural spring. This was commonplace in rural areas. Preparing the food for the animals, and a host of other rural household activities, which she speaks of with affection – I would have loved those years, and the opportunity of continuing a farming life which her parents had. Still, there was the risk of being called up for war in those days, and I always think that older people tend to think the old days were always better. My taste and experience of rural life whilst growing up has certainly been a pleasure, and has given me a richness in the understanding and appreciation of nature so strong that I believe it is largely responsible for my being able to cope with what life has thrown at me along the way.

The farm, though, as I mentioned earlier, was a small one, and to support the family my grandparents, both being hardworking people, had to go out to work. My grandfather was a case maker at "Riley's", a sweet factory in Halifax. My grandma was a spinner at a mill called "Peel House Gate" in the valley bottom. Mum was a weaver in a mill on the other side of the valley called "Murgatroyds" and has often pointed out to me the route which she used to take across the fields. The mill where she worked was on an enormous scale and gave employment to families all over the valley. It was built of stone but, unlike other mills up and down the valley, it did not give the grimy, depressed feeling of the North's industrial work. Instead, it stood majestically, yet somehow serenely, on the hillside and only came into view within a few miles of being approached. Locals would use it as a landmark in conversation whilst describing the area. Unfortunately, it suffered two fires in the late 1980s, the second destroying a large proportion of the mill and bringing it to a final close. I am sure most local people will remember it with either architectural interest or affectionately because a member of their family worked there.

The three sisters were all very attractive, and it was inevitable that my grandparents had lots of young men visiting the farm or rather, visiting the ladies. Eventually,

Mum aged 20 in her wedding dress. Mum married at the Registry Office.

Sister Margaret with husband John. Luddenden Church.

Sister Rita with husband George. Luddenden Church.

they were all to be married. My Auntie Margaret, the eldest, joined the Land Army, where she met my Uncle John, who was a Londoner. Auntie Rita married a local lad, my Uncle George, and mum married a local lad called Harry.

Some years later, still tending to the animals on the farm, my grandparents were finding life difficult. The doctor advised my grandfather, because of ill health, to give up the farm. This was a big wrench for him because of his love for animals. It seems that my Auntie Rita had some influence over them by this time, and encouraged them to move down into the bottom of the valley. And so the farm was given up and my grandparents moved into a cottage on "Brook Terrace", a row of cottages in the valley.

By this time mum had settled further down the valley in a cottage at Mytholmroyd, where her first child, Larry, my elder brother, was born in 1951. Unfortunately, his father was, to say the least, a difficult husband. He was in the Merchant Navy; I'm not sure of his position, but when home on leave he gave mum a rough time. This, apparently, was due to a weakness of his – alcohol. Mum persevered and tried hard to save the marriage, though in the end, having to endure violence, was persuaded by friends and her parents to leave him.

Returning to her parents, who caringly took her back home, she could see how my grandfather had not settled in their new home and was at a loss without animals to tend to. He had apparently mentioned at some time that he would like a public house. One day, unbeknown to my grandparents, my mother, on hearing of a tenancy becoming vacant, filled in an application form on behalf of my grandparents. A short while after, much to mum's joy and to my grandparents' astonishment, there was a reply to say my grandparents had been chosen and would they go along for an interview. Mum tells me she had a bit of a ticking-off by my grandma, recalling her words, 'Walt', as she always referred to my grandad, 'Look what our Laura's gone and done!'

My grandparents took up the offer, and within a short while moved in to become landlord and landlady of "The Waggoner's Rest" inn at Wainstalls, high on the valley side, above Luddenden. This was a public house situated about half a mile further up the valley, on the opposite side to where their old farm had been. It was a brewery-owned pub, as they nearly all were in those days, which, for the benefit of people that know the area, was called "Ramsden's", situated at Wards End in Halifax, where the new Halifax Building Society Headquarters now stand. The pub had panoramic views across the valley, and also enjoyed with it several acres of land. Needless to say, my grandfather was making plans for new livestock, and before long had some eleven or twelve dairy cows, along with pigs, goats, horses, dogs, cats, hens, ducks and geese. He was in his glory.

Aerial Photograph of the Waggoners Rest Pub in beautiful picturesque valley of Luddenden, on the Pennines of Yorkshire, where my early childhood memories began.

In those days pubs did not have catering facilities, and the most they served in the way of food was packets of crisps, plain only, with a small blue bag of salt included, and packets of peanuts. On domino nights, my grandparents would lay on pie and peas, with no charge. This would be in the Tap Room, a room where ladies were strictly forbidden.

By now, my mother was courting strongly with an extremely kind and jolly character called Teddy, whom I was to have the pleasure of meeting some years later. However, whatever effect my mother's previous husband's behaviour had on her, which she says it had, after several proposals of marriage from Teddy, she one day decided to tell him she did not want to see him again, thus ending the relationship. This left Teddy heartbroken and he apparently told my mother that, if he could not marry her, he would never marry anyone else, and to this day he is still single.

Some time after, there were some road works being carried out by the Water Board just above "The Waggoner's Rest". The workmen made frequent visits to the pub for drinks and one of them, a Ukrainian named Michael, asked my mother to go out with him. My mother agreed after the consent and instructions of her parents, who were very protective as to whom she kept company with. They had also taken a great liking to Teddy, and were extremely saddened as well as angry with mother that she had turned him down as her future husband.

Shortly into her relationship with Michael she became pregnant, much to my grandparents' horror; they were very strict and, to a certain extent, Victorian in their way of thinking. They were a respectful family and, in those days, to have a baby when not married was frowned upon. My grandmother apparently encouraged my mother to get rid of the baby before it was born. They were about to be disgraced. I can understand how they must have felt in those days. However, my mother refused, and nine months later an illegitimate baby boy was born, by definition "a bastard" – it was me.

My father, being a Ukrainian, wanted to call me Stephan, but my mother wanted me to have an English Christian name, as my surname was going to be Ukrainian. They compromised by calling me Stephen, as in Steven, and I was eventually christened Stephen Onyskiw.

My father loved mum very much, and I think she must have loved him. He worked very hard to provide a home, taking a job in a brickyard, which used to operate up Beacon Hill, just out of Halifax. He was proud of his work and earned good money there, though for long hours. He was also willing to take on mum's first-born, so mum left her parents' home at the pub to go into their own home near Halifax.

Mum tells me my father would give her anything she wanted. There were obviously good times, and mum speaks of my father introducing her to his Ukrainian friends, and of becoming familiar with certain foods and customs. Also, according to mum, my father was very jealous of her, and always wanted a report if she had ventured out without him.

At this point, I must tell you that I begin to form my own opinions about mum, possibly because I am a little biased towards my father, and feel he had not had a fair chance. I find the word "jealous" a very difficult one to fit into my vocabulary. I don't like it, basically, because it means playing with someone's feelings, usually in a hurtful way, and it could be dangerous. At what point in a couple's relationship does one become jealous as opposed to being caring? Once referred to as "jealous", then surely the other person must own up to the actions which brought the jealousy about.

Mum has made no secret to me whilst I've been growing up of the happenings between her and my father, and told me of a time when she went out with a friend and told my father what time she would be home. In fact, she was hours later and sounded as though she had had a good time. Rightly or wrongly, my father acted in a so-called "jealous" way. Apparently, he was furious with her, though I want to believe that it was through genuine concern for her safety.

As time went by, mum found my father too strict to live with. There were, at times, raging tempers. One day, mum decided to leave whilst my father was at work, taking me and eventually gaining custody over me. Shortly after my father insisted he was taking me to Italy to live with his new Italian wife. It was much harder in those days for a father to take custody of his child, particularly if there was no marriage.

Yet again, mum returned home; now with two children. As strict as my grandparents were, I was accepted into the family under the condition that I was christened before entering their house, as my grandmother was very superstitious.

Adjoining the pub was a small cottage, and this was made ready for mum to live in. Things were not going to be easy. There was talk of my father bringing his Ukrainian friends up to the house to cause trouble, and my grandparents feared for my mother's life, and she was not allowed out for quite some time. At times I can almost feel my father's anguish at wanting to see his son, and it was a slow process of his coming to terms with the situation.

As the Court had ruled custody to mum over both children, the fathers were ordered to pay maintenance money towards our upbringing. This had to be collected weekly at the court in Halifax by mum.

In general children are not usually capable of remembering things until they are between three and four years old. I can remember certain happenings distinctly by this time, which were related to "The Waggoner's Rest" public house-cum-farm. Larry was now six years old and we were beginning to be company for each other. It seemed my grandparents thought a lot of Larry, and my grandfather particularly leaned to him, having lost his own son. They bought for him readily, and one thing in his favour was that he was not a bastard. I recall a set of wooden skittles bought for his birthday, varnished, with red rings painted round them, and two wooden balls to match. I remember them because I used to play with them on their sides, imitating grandad's cows, as if the round tops were their heads. There weren't such things as plastic farm animals in those days, though there were some metal ones, a few of which we later acquired. I remember the beautiful old brown patterned moquette sofa, with its two rolled arms, under one of which there was a wooden handle to adjust the position should my grandma wish to lower her head when lying down. It served as a huge screen for us to play behind with the skittles every Sunday afternoon when all the adults were brossan after their traditional Sunday lunch, and would sit round the roaring open fire with laughter and adult talk.

A very proud, but aggressive, black and white Muscovy drake used to pace up and down the farmyard by the roadside. His bill, with a bright red growth at the top, would alternately shoot forwards and then backwards whilst hissing. Although he was impressive, he was certainly intimidating enough for a three year old, and I can remember steering clear of him, heeding my grandparents' and mother's advice. Larry used to spend time in and out of the mistal, watching grandad tend to the cows. As I had never been allowed in there because I was too young, I recall some talk focused on my seeing the cows. Mum carried me into the mistal in her arms, my head turning this way and that in full observation. So vividly do I see now the strawberry roan cow which turned its head to look at us and, at the same time, let out an almighty roar. With a roar that was almost as loud as hers and floods of tears, I was taken back into the house.

An accident which occurred whilst on the farm is remembered just as vividly. Whilst playing a game of "follow my leader", with Larry leading, I was encouraged to jump off what seemed to be at the time a twenty-foot

The Waggoner's Rest Inn, Stocks Lane, Luddenden.

Me at Jim
Housans Trough
Farm, Stocks Lane,
Luddenden. 1957

Mum with Keith in
arms, Larry left, me
right at Jim Housans,
Trough Farm, Stocks
Lane, Luddenden.
1957

high wall. It resulted in my splitting my head open. With no telephones at home, I recall scenes of blood and friends being summoned to organise transport to take me to hospital; there I received stitches. It was a strange feeling when I returned as an adult to the scene of the accident to find that the wall was in fact only four feet high and was still there thirty-eight years on.

Looking back now, I feel I can recall those early years so vividly because I was enjoying the environment at the time. It was a start to life I think all children should have the opportunity of experiencing: animals, the fresh open air, the feel of nature, everything so tangible it is an ongoing adventure, helping to develop any child's mind and body in preparation for life ahead.

Unfortunately, this lifestyle was to be somewhat diluted for us, as mum's plans for the future took us away from the farm.

We look too high for things close by
And lose what nature found us;
For life hath here no charms so dear
As friends and home around us.
  (Whiteley Turner, "A Springtime Saunter")

Chapter Two

Almost three years had passed, and mum seemed to be willing to try another relationship. This time a local man, working as a fitter in the pub for the brewery "Ramsden's". He was of smart appearance, with a moustache, and always wore a trilby. His character was of a stern and disciplined type, a definite no-nonsense man, by the name of Furnist, twenty years mum's senior. When working away, he would take mum, Larry and me as a treat. It was probably against company rules. I can picture the old-fashioned, box-type, chocolate brown pick-up vehicle with its brewery emblem on the doors – a white threepenny bit shaped circle with dark blue centre, upon which there was a white "R" (Ramsden's). We would all squeeze onto the leather bench-type seat, and enjoy the journey ahead. Mum was very proud of us, and the fact that we were well behaved whilst not having a father was reflected on her.

I can remember one public house Furnist took us to had what seemed at the time a very plush interior. Before he started work, we were seated on a bar stool and treated to a packet of crisps. I can remember feeling so privileged, and as though I was being tested, and also my manners. Looking back, I know my own father would have given me treats of that kind if he had had the chance.

Quite often on these journeys Furnist would take us on a scenic detour, calling at his parents' home; a railway property right beside the level crossing at Pately Bridge in the Yorkshire Dales. The excitement of these visits was almost too much to bear. On entering the room his mother, a small old lady in her eighties, never to be seen without a cigarette, would approach us with all the joy and hospitality that she would have shown if we were her own family. There were drinks and sweets, but most of all I remember a beautifully black leaded fireplace, in front of which lay the most colourful rug which she had made herself from bits of material. I enjoyed these visits so much that I only ever wanted to go on his journeys when there was a Pately Bridge detour.

Before very long mum had left her cottage at "The Waggoner's Rest" to set up home with Furny, as she now called him. This was in an area just outside Halifax called Ovenden Way. Within the next three years mum bore two more sons, now to Furny. The eldest was Keith Anton; the younger was Darren. It seems that, before meeting Furny, mum had developed a very strong maternal instinct, and was quite happy with the way she was dealing with her children. Now, Keith and Darren's father wanted to show his authority. His behaviour towards all four children became upsetting for mum, and she speaks of him becoming violent. This led to visits from a Cruelty Inspector, who eventually advised her to leave Furny and go back to her parents.

Left to right Larry, Keith, Mum, Darren, Me age 4. 1958

By now, mum had realised she could no longer return to her parents, as this would be too much to put upon them. So the Cruelty Inspector made arrangements for mum to move into a council flat at Mixenden, on the outskirts of Halifax. It was from this home that I started my school days. These were to be spent at an infant school a few miles away at Wainstalls. Without taking into account the purpose of schools this one, for me, was ideally situated, high on the Pennines, in open country. There was a strict, but very nice headmistress, Mrs Midgley. The only other member of staff I recall was a dinner lady by the name of Mrs Riley, known to all the pupils as "Old Ma Riley", for she was a formidable woman, who watched over us at play times with such contempt that I wondered why she ever worked with children at all. When her brass bell rang at the end of play a line was formed almost instantly in utter silence, whilst heads were counted. On occasions, I dared to be the last in the line, after trying to drag myself away from the most beautiful black carthorse that used to hang his head over a wall that surrounded our playing field adjoining the playground whilst I smothered him with affection, and fed him handfuls of grass that always tastes sweeter on the other side.

For my elder brother Larry, there were less fond memories of that school, as he reminded me on several occasions whilst growing up. He was to endure the embarrassment of being summoned by "Old Ma Riley" to be told, in front of his class, to take his younger brother home, as I had suffered a toilet accident and had no clothes to change into. After making a quick exit, he would scold me whilst walking to the bus stop to catch our bus home.

There were still visits to my grandparents, though these were becoming less frequent. By now I was old enough to remember the occasional visit into the Tap Room, where I recall the clatter of ivory dominoes on the old wood-topped tables with intricate wrought iron legs, on which stood round glass ashtrays with the wording "Ramsden's Stone

Trough Ales".

The flat where we now lived in Mixenden, in contrast to my grandparents' home, was on a housing estate and we were on the second floor. I remember mum leaving Larry in charge at times, when she would quickly visit a neighbour. This allowed us to gain amusement by a little mischief in emptying all the newspapers out of the television cupboard, and picking out the funniest pieces. These were always out of bounds to us, as the "Beano" and "Dandy" were more suitable reading for our age. I cannot remember Keith or Darren waking up at any time on these occasions, and we always had instructions as to which neighbour we should go to if help was needed.

A sight, which became very familiar over the years, was mum standing over Keith and Darren with a safety pin in her mouth, whilst pushing another one very efficiently into a nappy in the process of changing one of them. This was always done with us by her side and eventually we had to help not only with this, but with all aspects of domestic chores; and I mean all. The nappies were terry towelling ones in those days and with no washing machine, had to be boiled. The kitchen would be full of steam whilst, in turn, we would help mum to put nappies from the steaming tub through a free standing wringing machine. I can hear her talking now with relief and sheer pride of how clean she could get her nappies, which was with the aid of an item called "Dolly Blue" left in the boil. This was always included in our regular errands to the local shop.

The council flat was on a large red brick housing estate, mainly occupied by large families of kids. "Kids" seems a more appropriate word when they live in this kind of area. Living in a less populated area they would be referred to as children, along with a little class distinction. If anyone was to ask me what made me tick? What was my purpose for living? What gave me ultimate comfort in life? It would be a simple answer of fauna and flora. There is nothing before, and nothing after rural life for me, almost as though each encounter with nature is building me as I go through life; be it to feel the elements from one season to another; to sharing my life with some four-legged friend or just observing and absorbing the sheer beauty of scenery which surrounds us in this world. Had my umbilical cord been cut from the root of some shrub, I could not feel a greater closeness to nature.

Although the area of the council estate where we lived fell somewhere between suburbia and rural, the immediate vicinity offended me, even at this early age. Row after row of houses looking at each other, each one deprived of a view of nature, almost of their own identity by similarity. That was until the occupants would appear who, although they were all from a similar poor financial background, certainly had their own identities. So impressed was I by these strong characters that I have vivid memories of such persons as Ada Luck. Ada was our next-door neighbour, never to be seen without a turban, which fastened in a knot just above her brow, exposing one of her hair curlers and producing two lugs which stuck out and, to my mind, looked so ridiculous that I imagined some form of human rabbit with displaced ears. This was matched with a floral wraparound apron covering all except her arms, which her rolled-up sleeves exposed. She was a buxom woman, who seemed to have been put on this earth to scrub and clean alone. I recall mum and her borrowing bags of sugar and pints of milk from each other. This seemed to happen a lot in those days, almost a custom within these densely populated communities. Then there was Fay Gibbons, a woman of slight stature, supporting her candy-floss-like bleached blonde hair style with contrasting bright red lipstick and wearing an imitation leopard skin coat, as she strutted around on high-heeled shoes for work and leisure. She lived in what was called "The Circle" on the estate, known to be a less desirable place to live.

There is always a very strong grapevine in these communities, some taking more notice of it than others, and the person at the beginning of this one was Winnie Blackburn. Living directly opposite us, she was constantly in and out of our house with the local gossip; whether fabricated or true, she took great delight in knowing everyone's affairs.

Well, these are just a few people that come to mind, but the whole community was like "Coronation Street" on a massive scale. Once in a while sparks would fly as a mother would be upset by a day's happenings, and in turn voices would be raised around the area until pandemonium was reached, with children and adults shouting and screaming, usually in defence of their own families and territories.

My release, as I saw it, from these surroundings, was my days spent at Wainstalls Infant and Junior School. Larry and I would travel there by bus, which would be full of schoolchildren. I used to like the side seat, which was at the rear end of the bus by the open entrance; I could always see more of the scenery from there as it was higher than the other seats. On these journeys we became friendly with one of the regular bus conductors who was always generous with sweets and humour. At the front of the bus was a glass-covered device which, at intervals, revealed a different flap on which there was advertising of some product. One of these became very popular with the schoolchildren, and as the flap dropped to reveal its advert we would all shout at the top of our voices, 'Stardrops' to the attractive dark blue background with white stars and a yellow tornado-type character, advertising a house carpet cleaner. The bus conductor, who eventually we came to know as Billy, would love to hear us all. We would speak of Billy to mum and on occasions she would come with us to school. These occasions became more regular, and it wasn't long before Billy was visiting our home, and the friendship between mum and he became more serious.

One morning, as mum was preparing us for school, she had the unfortunate experience of finding a man in the toilet. Somehow, in a state of shock, she grabbed the children

Billy (Paula's Dad) with Mum, me on left Larry in foreground and Keith with Mum on right. On holiday in Skegness (about 1960).

and fled the house, screaming in the process as she reached one of her neighbours. What had happened was that whilst having a visitor the evening before, mum had left the door unlocked; normally it was always kept locked. A man, who apparently knew mum lived alone, entered and stayed in the house until the visitor had gone; continuing to stay once we were all asleep. When the Police were informed and mum had to go before an identity parade, it turned out that the man in question was a policeman, and he was immediately thrown out of the Police Force. By the way, the neighbour mum ran to was Winnie Blackburn. You can imagine what that did for the grapevine.

The incident had unnerved mum in the house and Billy, who lived by himself nearer to Halifax, also owned another house close to town, and very kindly offered to let us live there. For me, if not the residents, the area was more true to "Coronation Street" than ever; I hated it. However, we were not to live there for very long as Billy, who was Irish, came under increasing pressure from members of his very large family, who were very strong in Catholicism.

19

They constantly questioned him and tried to terminate his relationship with mum. Eventually, he decided to uproot us to get away from his family, taking us out of the area to live in a house in Balby, Doncaster, South Yorkshire. This house was where I begin to remember some of the worst experiences of my childhood.

A red brick house, at the end of a long road, in a depressed area, it had a long narrow yard to the rear, enclosed by a six to seven foot high red brick wall which, at one end, had a tall wooden gate that, at the least opportunity, I would unbolt to explore the surrounding area. Shortly after moving there mum became pregnant to Billy and, as her story goes, unwillingly.

By now Larry was old enough to go to middle school, and was sent to one just up the road from where we lived. I was sent to one about one mile away and recall standing crying and petrified in the playground on my first day, as a teacher tried to coax me inside. It was the first time I had come into contact with coloured people – which, along with moving house into a new area and changing schools, was difficult to accept in those days, coming from an area with all local people. However, one Pakistani girl, much older than myself, by the name of Naznime, befriended me and made the days ahead a little easier but the area was urban – totally urban – and the environment crushed me. When was I to see my grandparents again?

Larry was also upset by the move. In the home, as the months went by, the domestic scene was deteriorating rapidly. It is amazing how two people can have such an effect on each other to the extent that, looking back, I could hardly recognise them for who they were before they met.

Mum had gone into deep depression through the pregnancy. I recall her gaunt look and lack of interest in herself, whilst she continued to wear a pea green mohair-type coat as her delivery day got nearer. Billy, who had taken a job as a caretaker at a school, was becoming extremely bad-tempered and would refuse to let mum out of the house. I recall him refusing to let Larry watch television and at night he would come into my bedroom and wake me up, saying that it was all my fault that he and mum were not happy. This was the man who used to give us sweets, and laugh and joke with us as a bus conductor.

There were lots of visits from his family, and on one occasion I remember them standing out in the street in heated discussion with Billy, whilst mum was inside with us, watching from the window. This pressure from his family brought constant arguments indoors, making mum feel a lesser person.

By now, my grandparents had retired from "The Waggoner's Rest" inn on their doctor's advice, due to grandad's ill health. On the doctor's recommendation they had moved south to a beautiful bungalow just outside a market town called Spilsby, in Lincolnshire. This was a beautiful area, and a beneficial move for them. However, grandad was somewhat disappointed that he was not seeing his eldest grandson grow up as often as he would like and, on Larry's birthday, a beautiful brand-new, blue, two-wheeled bike which they had bought for him, was delivered by train to our home in Doncaster. This caused great excitement and, although I was too small for it and had not been taught to ride a bike, I was occasionally allowed to sit on the saddle whilst Larry pushed me along.

All this time mum had never mentioned her pregnancy to her parents, and knew as time was going on it was getting harder. Eventually, we all took a trip down to Lincolnshire to visit my grandparents and for mum to break the news of the new arrival. This, she feared, was going to be difficult, which proved to be the case. My grandparents were yet again shamed and found the situation difficult to tolerate. After much discussion, my grandparents refused to recognise the baby unless mum agreed to marry Billy. So, against mum's wishes, finally admitting she wasn't in love with him, Billy was asked to join us.

Over a period of about one week, whilst we stayed with them, there were heated discussions and arrangements were made for mum and Billy to be married at the Register Office in Spilsby. The green mohair coat, which mum had worn constantly throughout her pregnancy, was replaced with a thick brown beaver skin coat of grandma's to wear to the Register Office. I recall watching from the window of the bungalow as the party made its way down the road for what should have been a happy occasion.

Shortly after, back in Doncaster, on the 29th April 1962, mum gave birth to a baby girl. Mum had now taken Billy's surname by marriage, and so the baby was named Paula Finlay. Billy's family were furious, and his elder brother refused to see him again. Life became unbearable for all of us, though mum had regained a more stable state of mind since the baby was born and became much stronger in herself again. As each day went by, she was becoming more independent, fending for her now five children, and resenting Billy, who had now become known to us as "Bill", more and more.

Bill was working on night shift at the school as caretaker and mum used to talk to Larry and me after he had gone to work, and reassure us that we would all one day be free of him and go back to Halifax. On discussing this with a neighbour, who was very good to mum and said she did not know how she dare go about trying to leave Bill, mum's plan went into action one night after Bill had gone to work. We were told that, the next day, after he had gone to work, we would help mum to pack bare essentials and take a taxi to the train station. So, on that evening, we were all put to bed as usual and Bill went to work at about 10.00 p.m. When he had gone, mum came up, woke us all, and prepared us to leave. Finally, a note was written and left on the mantelpiece, which I can visualise to this day.

Once at the train station, we all mounted the train in which we sat very nervously wondering if Bill had somehow found out and would reach us before the train pulled out. Eventually, the whistle blew and as the train pulled out, mum said, *'Well, he can't get us now.'* I have never experienced such a bewildering feeling in all my life. It was a mixture of a sense of freedom, escape, security, and yet not knowing where on earth we were going to spend the night. Mum told us she was going to take us to the house of a lady with whom she had become great friends whilst living with my father; this lady became known to us as "Auntie Florence".

A tall, frail figure of about six foot, suffering from severe asthma, Auntie Florence, who was a spinster, lived in a ground floor flat with a white poodle by the name of Kimmy in Sowerby Bridge, West Yorkshire. At around one o'clock in the morning we all stood outside her door whilst mum knocked and called out to let her know who we were. As she answered the door, her high-pitched voice screamed out in amazement and surprise as she beckoned us all inside.

With mum carrying a newborn baby, we all helped to prepare a drawer, which Auntie Florence had taken out of her sideboard, to be used as a bed for Paula. Keith and Darren slept on the sofa, and Larry and I slept on the floor, whilst Auntie Florence listened eagerly to mum giving her all the up-to-date events, as we all settled down to sleep.

Chapter Three

After mum's marriage to Bill, his family refused to recognise it as, according to their religion, they were still "living in sin" because they had married in a register office. Mum had told them that she already had a home before she met Bill, and he should provide another one for her so they could part. Bill's family were in agreement with this, and being so afraid of them, particularly of his elder brother, arrangements were made for him to fly back to his parents' home in Ireland for cash to purchase a house.

Within a few weeks we said "goodbye" to Auntie Florence, and moved into a semi-detached house, which Bill had provided, at the top of several rows of streets, in an area called Spring Edge, King Cross, Halifax. These have since been demolished to make way for new housing development.

The house and situation was an improvement on our previous addresses, and faced south overlooking the local, what we called in those days, "rec." (playground). It had a large living-kitchen cellar, which backed on to some outside toilets adjacent to the houses in the street behind. This room became the most functional room of the house, unfortunately for me, as the upstairs had quite a pleasant view. It had a black lead "Yorkist" range fireplace, where mum used to prepare meals, boil water on the fire and air our clothes on the creel above.

I was now seven years old, Larry was eleven, Keith was five, Darren was three and Paula was just a few months old. Mum had chosen this particular house with schools in mind, which was the next thing for her to attend to. Conveniently situated less than half a mile away were two schools – Haugh Shaw Junior and Haugh Shaw Secondary Modern schools. Larry was to go to the secondary and I was to go to the junior, just across the road. We were introduced to the headmasters and teachers, and I felt as far as schools go, I was going to be reasonably happy here.

Mum had, in the past few years, been troubled by Keith's general progress and had contacted someone in the medical profession for advice as he was now of school age. Mum noticed that, over the years, Keith could not control one of his eyes properly; it kept wandering independently into the corner. Tests were carried out, and eventually mum was told that Keith had what they called a "lazy eye". Along with this, they found that Keith was generally slow at school, and after further educational tests, mum was advised to send Keith to a "special" school.

Keith was a very happy-go-lucky child, easygoing and carefree. He had a particularly healthy complexion, and in company was very shy. Due to his nature, he was a victim of bullying; this began at a very early age in the home. When mum eventually registered Keith with a special school a few miles away, because he was not "streetwise", transport had to be arranged to take him to and from school. This was in the form of what was called a "Corporation car", which used to draw up outside our house, shining black with the Halifax Corporation coat of arms on the driver's door, and the most patient chauffeur, who became a real pal to all the children, including Keith, whom he had to collect.

On Keith's first morning, I remember us all feeling sorry for him as mum prepared him for school, and we all made a particular effort to encourage him and say how envious we were of him having a lovely car to go to school in. With a wry smile and his carefree nature, he easily accepted the situation.

As the years went by I enjoyed school very much, though

I came to realise that there was a distinct lack of interest by mum in my schoolwork and activities. When parents' evenings came round, she would send a note with me to give to the teacher, sometimes quite strongly worded as to why she could or would not go. I was proud of my work, and in particular one lesson we had in junior school called "Craft Lesson", where we made our own hardback for a notepad, on which we had to make our own design from a marbling technique we were shown. This I thoroughly enjoyed and came top of the class with my design, which was to be shown on Parents' Evening. After pleading with mum to attend, I would be told, *'No, it's alright, I will see it when you bring it home.'* The notes were sent regularly, and it hurt deeply to hand them to the teacher, as I would with great embarrassment, knowing that all the other children were going to have their parents there.

But the embarrassment did not just come with the notes. Back at home mum had begun to find her feet again. We were all at school and she had only Paula to look after during the day now. At teatime, after school, we would all help to prepare for tea: running errands to the corner shop and helping to fill the zinc bath in which we all took turns in front of the coal fire; there was no central heating. When we had all finished, Larry and myself used to help bath Paula, who had her own pink plastic bath. After this operation a crisp, clean, fresh-smelling flannelette nightie was taken from a wooden clotheshorse, which stood beside the fire where our pyjamas had also been aired. Although there were grumbles and moans about this exercise as mum would comb our hair, I remember the satisfying and refreshed feeling that followed, giving us second wind for play before bed, only to be told, *'No! Up them stairs!'* Winter and summer alike, it was mum's aim to have us all in bed for six o'clock, and she carried this out without exception, of which she reminds me to this day.

We were soon to learn that she wanted the evenings to herself. I could understand adults being tired and wanting a rest, but we knew our cousin Robert, who was Auntie Rita and Uncle George's son, and friends of ours did not go to bed at six o'clock every night. Then I became aware it was not so much the fact I was going to bed early that troubled me, but what mum was doing with her time in the evenings. Arrangements were being made for Auntie Florence to babysit; on occasions there would be friends of mum's who she thought she could trust to leave with us. Impossible as it was to go to sleep so early, I recall having pillow fights with my brothers and making mischief whilst mum would be getting ready to go out. We would listen behind the bedroom door, or even dare to go onto the landing, as mum would give her instructions to the babysitter. This would be followed by a trip upstairs to check if we were asleep. I knew if she found us still awake she would scold us, but I was usually prepared to take this risk so I could see what she looked like before she went out.

From left, Larry, Mum with Paula on her knee, myself, front left Keith, and front right Darren (Spring Edge, King Cross, Halifax 1963/1964).

Now in her mid-thirties, mum was very attractive; her clothes were complementary of both her attractiveness and her figure, and were immaculate. I can remember in detail her cosmetics because I watched her spend hours tending her face with Max Factor "Tempting Touch" powder, which came in a pale blue compact. Also, the experienced movement of her hand as it went from left to right across her lips with a lipstick; to be followed by a drawn-in action of her lips, which I always found amusing. Her beautifully groomed, shoulder-length hair, which we had to take turns in combing, had been styled at the front by means of two metal grips, which created a series of waves, held in place by hair lacquer. All this was finally topped up with the fragrance of a perfume by the name of "Eau de Cologne" 711, which came in a tiny black bottle with a black cap and was packaged in a turquoise and gold box. As she would tuck in our bedclothes and bid us goodnight, I would ask where she was going, usually getting an evasive response. The smell of those cosmetics would linger for hours after she left the room. When visiting my grandparents, my grandfather would say aloud, in his broad Yorkshire accent, *'Hey up Gladys, our Laura's getting 'er war paint on ageeun.'* It was the early sixties and she was often complimented on how she had been taken for a teenager.

Though mum and Bill had parted, because he owned the house, and was still married to mum, he felt he still had rights over her. His frequent visits to the house were unwelcome, and as he insisted mum should not have any men friends staying there, this provoked her and, in turn, by ignoring this, her relationship with any man made Bill extremely .... yes! That word I find so difficult, "jealous". Consequently, this made for trouble, lots of trouble. Bill decided to watch the house day and night, making us feel like prisoners. I remember mum huddled up with us all in one room, keeping us deadly quiet whilst she listened for noises outside in the evenings. He often tried to force entry because mum would not see him. The windows had wooden shutters on the inside, which were folded out to use as blackouts in the war. These were secured with a metal bar, and mum used them often. A cousin of mum's, who was in the Police Force, and of whom she was very fond, used to call, *'As a deterrent for Bill,'* she would tell us, which was partially true, but I was reading between the lines now.

At lunch times, Larry would walk home from school for his lunch, and bring with him his school friends. By the time he reached his last year in school, some of his friends were quite mature and showed much interest in mum. Knowing her circumstances, they began to visit regularly. I hated their presence, and began to feel protective towards mum. Sometimes Bill would visit whilst they were there. There would be violent scenes, which we would witness. On one occasion I recall being narrowly missed by a missile thrown by mum at Bill, as I ducked down behind a chair; later I found it was an elaborate brass clock which he had bought her in the past.

One day, very suddenly, I was to have what seemed to me like a blackout. As I came round, feeling quite weak, I was told my behaviour had been somewhat aggressive – quite out of character for me, as I was a very quiet child. Mum was concerned, and as this recurred, she thought I was having some kind of fit and took me to the doctor who, in turn, sent me to see various specialists for tests. In the meantime, my aunties and uncles, my grandparents and other relatives and friends would insist there was nothing the matter with me that a stable family life would not cure. Over a period of twelve months, at the age of ten, the doctors could not find any reason for these blackouts and, fortunately, they only lasted for twelve months. However, this problem, along with raising her other children, and the difficult matrimonial circumstances, led mum to take advice from the authorities dealing with such cases, who said that they would make arrangements for me to go into a home for a while, in order to allow her a period of rest.

I was to find myself delivered to what seemed to me like a preparation camp for army recruits, in a place called Home Moss, Alderly Edge in Cheshire. It turned out that the children and adolescents there were being disciplined for bad behaviour and were from unstable backgrounds. There was a strict daily routine of how to look after oneself, from tending your bed in the dormitory; teeth cleaning; washing; cleaning your boots – these were army boots, which we had to wear on a parade every morning and through the day; to helping with meals served up until suppertime. These duties were carried out under the eye of a matron who put the fear of hell into you.

I was terrified and totally confused as to why I was in this kind of home, as I felt as though I was being punished. Mum was allowed to visit once a month. On her first visit, I think she was as surprised as me as to why I had been placed in this kind of establishment and was very upset.,she told me it was going to be difficult to get me out, as she had signed an official form for a set length of time. To my astonishment, she brought my clothes with her, asked me to get changed quickly, and we made a speedy exit through the grounds to the bus which had been provided for the visitors. I had cried every night for three weeks, and felt such relief – and comfort from the thought that mum had not forgotten me.

She consoled me as we chatted on the journey home by telling me that I would never have to return there. But even as she spoke, I was wondering what had been happening at home. It had seemed a long time. Were there many changes and, above all, was it going to be more peaceful, just mum and us again?

Shortly after I arrived home, a lady friend of mum's from across the green called to see how I was getting on and, knowing I was fond of animals, encouraged mum to buy me a rabbit. On agreeing, mum allowed a simple tea chest to be made into a rabbit hutch with the help of one of Larry's school friends. His father worked for the local dairy at

King Cross, and drove a wagon collecting full milk churns in exchange for empty ones, very early in the morning to farms over in Lancashire. He told me he knew of a farmer who had some young rabbits for sale and asked if I would like to go with him to choose one. This I did with the utmost urgency and excitement. I cannot quite remember but I don't think I had to pay because the milkman knew the farmer. It was a beautifully marked black and white rabbit, my very own pet but, unfortunately, did not live very long.

I was soon to learn that Larry's school friend, whose father was the milk wagon driver, was mum's new lover. This was a shock to me. Partly because I did not want her to have another man – I used to think of my own father – but mainly because of the embarrassment I had to endure at school. This young teenager had only left school a couple of years before Larry. They seemed very happy and the relationship seemed very serious. However, divorce was a long process in those days, and there were complications with Bill being a Catholic.

I was back at school for only a short time before starting secondary school across the road; Larry was almost ready for leaving secondary school.

The family income was pitiful, the main source coming from our three fathers in the way of "maintenance money", which was paid by them into the Magistrates' Court in Halifax. This had to be collected by mum every week; she would take us with her to join the long queue of mothers that stretched for about fifty yards down the entrance steps and round the building; all the women had the same look of anticipation on their faces, which now and then disappeared as they tried to keep their children in tow. Slowly, very slowly, the line would move forward; it was boredom at its worst. As we got nearer to the counter, we would hear mum comment in sympathy, as a mother was told by the cashier that there was no money for her. Mum had got to know the lady at the counter very well through her visits, and I remember her pleasant manner; she was a smart clerical type with glasses, by the name of Joyce. As it was our turn to approach the counter, Joyce would nod her head, either 'yes' with a smile, or 'no' with a sorrowful look as mum received the bad news. I think that in this regard mum was quite fortunate, as our fathers very rarely missed payments.

Then there were State benefits, to which families in our circumstances were entitled. Free milk was one I can remember, but this is not an area which I favour. As for the various means of financial help, I have never been able to (but probably because I never wanted to) really understand them. I realise mum could not have raised us all without these means, but I have very strong feelings about this. I believe in a fair day's work for a fair day's pay and, although there are people who genuinely do not have control over their destiny in life, fortunately most of us do and should therefore be responsible for our own financial status. I don't wish to dwell on this, as I have had a lifetime's experience and keep coming up with the same answer – work.

Holidays were out of the question, but there were visits to our grandparents in the main school holidays, which I think were a lifeline to us all.

For a reason I cannot quite remember, an acquaintance of Bill's, by the name of Bert, who sympathised with mum's position, used to give us all a lift down to Lincoln in his old Morris Traveller, as mum could not afford the train fare. I recall arguments as to who were going to be the two to lie in the back, as there was a sense of independence about being furthest away from mum, who was in the passenger seat. Also, we could lie down with a pillow and would fall asleep knowing we had been told the journey was a long one. I'm sure, with today's motoring laws, we would not have got very far without a Police check for the back doors were fastened with string, and seat belts were not on the scene. I seem to think Bert had a relative or some work to attend to in Lincoln. However, we were very grateful for the lifts.

From Lincoln we used to catch a double-decker bus. This was a treat in itself, as the buses, with their shiny, bottle green paintwork and plush moquette seats, were in much better condition than the West Yorkshire ones. Mum would seat us all in a line at the front, on one seat, along with a strict warning that we had not to speak until we arrived at our destination. There were comments from other passengers in amazement at how well-behaved we were. Little did they know it was more than our holiday was worth to do otherwise.

The bus used to stop just past my grandparents' bungalow, which was on a busy main road to the seaside resort of Skegness. As we walked down the garden path towards the door, which was always open, allowing coloured plastic streamers to keep the flies out, tempting food smells would greet us of the kind that only grandparents seem to be able to make. There would be much excitement as my grandparents welcomed us indoors. Within minutes we would be asking to go out into the garden, knowing we would get grandad's approval, as he was so proud of his garden. The main attraction for us was an extremely faithful sheepdog by the name of Lassie; she was tethered by a chain in one corner of the garden. My grandparents had taken her with them from "The Waggoner's Rest" but found they could not let her loose in their new home as the main road was too dangerous and Lassie, being a farm dog, was not used to the traffic.

The garden was paradise: well stocked and maintained, with an abundance of dahlias, nasturtiums, stocks, lupins, roses etc. The bungalow was detached, and the flowers bordered the lawns along the front and down each side, with a large vegetable garden to the rear. We would eat the sweetest peas straight from the pod whilst picking them for the Sunday dinner. Broad beans, lettuce, beetroot, radishes, potatoes and onions would all be neatly growing in rows leading up to a strawberry patch that was beside a large compost heap which, when filled with lawn clippings, we would take turns at diving into. Silver snail trails were to be found early in the mornings, and we would follow them to see who could find the largest snail.

Grandad was of medium build, with pure white hair and only one leg. He had lost his other leg fighting in the First World War, in 1914, in Ypres, and learned to walk with an artificial one. My grandma was a frailer figure, with little interest in animals. This meant neither of them would take Lassie for walks, as she was quite boisterous and strong. However, my grandparents became very friendly with a lady by the name of Miss Rixen, a middle-aged spinster, who worked next door at "The Shades Hotel". Miss Rixen became not just a friend to Lassie, but was absolutely besotted by her, and vice versa. Every day Miss Rixen took Lassie for a walk, and every day Lassie instinctively would begin to get excited, panting minutes before she was due to arrive. Larry and I were allowed to go with them and once across the busy road, Miss Rixen would walk us down a long field called The Avenue, with trees at either side, and cattle grazing in plenty. Once off the lead, Lassie would have the time of her life, whilst Miss Rixen would tell us stories. This usually finished by Lassie rolling in a cow clap, which resulted in Miss Rixen hosing her down back at the hotel, much to all our enjoyment. She would then take us inside and refresh Larry and me with a glass of "pop", whilst Lassie was always given the biggest knucklebone she could find from the kitchen. Lassie would carry this back proudly to the bungalow, tail wagging with sheer pleasure.

In the summer holidays we would often stay down there for quite a few weeks, this giving us time to be adventurous and explore things and places a little "out of bounds" to us. Larry was becoming sort of grown-up and did not like to be seen with his younger brother now. As he made his way into the market town, he began to make friends and was allowed to go a little further afield. After several attempts at running after him and his gang, and being rejected, I would go in the opposite direction alone, which eventually led me into the country, where I came across a large dairy farm owned by a family called the Dennits. I became very friendly with all the workpeople there, and would spend hours making dens amongst the hay bales in the Dutch barn and, eventually, milked my first cow by hand – an old, lame Friesian by the name of Magnolia. On returning home after milking time, I would walk down the garden path sporting the healthiest tanned complexion from the day's sun, feeling a sense of joy and fulfilment with what the day had offered me, and wanting to share it with someone, yet wanting to keep it a secret at the same time.

As we were summoned for tea, we would be taken to the kitchen sink to have our hands scrubbed. Meal times were always much more of an occasion at my grandparents, probably because they had more food than us. There was always much more preparation before eating than there was at home. I used to enjoy the orderly and disciplined way we were all seated round the table, as grandad would carve the meat whilst the sun would stream in through the window.

After eating, if the adults were in conversation we would be excused from the table only by the words – '*Please may I leave the table?*' – along with a clean plate. Then, making the most of the last hour of the day, I used to slink off out into the garden, perch myself on top of the wood-lapped fence which surrounded it, and watch them play bowls to the sweet smell of lawn clippings heating up in the compost heap below as the evening sun went down. Finally, our names would be called: '*Larry! Stephen! Come on, wash, bed!*'

To end the day in a bath (with taps) that we did not have to fill ourselves was as much a pleasure as the rest of the holiday. We would ask mum to be careful not to scrub too hard because of the tenderness but were also proud of the tan we had gained in the midday sun. Into bed, I settled down wishing this could last forever.

Grandad with me in garden of their bungalow in Spilsby, Lincolnshire. 1959–1960.

Chapter Four

After returning home at the end of one summer holiday, it was time for me to change schools. I wasn't unduly worried, just a little nervous about the size, though as I had not passed my Eleven-plus exam, Haugh Shaw Secondary School was only half the size of the grammar school. I remember my main concern distinctly, which was: having to discard my short trousers for long ones. This I managed to postpone for the first twelve months, but then, with remarks from Larry as to how silly it was for me to wear short trousers in the "big school", I was eventually encouraged to leave them and my braces behind, in exchange for some long ones, now to be supported by means of an elastic snake belt. I knew this was much more grown-up but how I missed the sun and fresh air on my legs.

Larry had built himself quite a reputation at school. This was not through the teachers and his work, but with a following of certain pupils, with whom he would share other interests, such as truancy, smoking, drinking – all these things he looked upon as "big boys' stuff". Now I was to enter his school, he was concerned that I would damage his image, as I did none of these things.

When mum first came to register us all for school, she realised there were going to be complications, as we all had different surnames. At the time she thought it would be kinder for us if we all had the same name. As she had no intention of staying married to Bill, Finlay was not a suitable surname. The fact that Larry was the first one into school meant that everyone knew his surname as Lockwood and referred to mum as "Mrs Lockwood", so that was the surname given to Keith, Darren and me, which we were to use for the rest of our lives. Paula was allowed to be called by her father's name, as she would go through school much later than us. Also in her favour was the fact that mum had married her father, as she had with Larry's.

One evening, when mum had decided Larry was old enough to babysit, she went out, leaving him in charge. This was an ideal opportunity for him to call in his friends. All acting in their so-called "grown-up" way – smoking, drinking, etc – they decided I should get used to this kind of behaviour and held me down to the ground, face up, whilst in turn they forced me to smoke a cigarette. As I resisted strongly enough, they eventually let me go. From then on I was regarded as a "sissy", making no allowances for the fact I was just a different character. The thought of a cigarette in my mouth almost choked me.

We were always brought up by mum to be known to each other as brothers and sister. Although she had never kept it a secret who our fathers were, and what had happened, we never really understood that we were, in fact, stepbrothers and stepsister.

Larry eventually left school with no particular interest and went from one job to another. Going through school I became interested in certain areas. I was doing exceptionally well at English, enjoying woodwork, geography and, particularly, gymnastics. When evening classes were offered to us for any of these subjects, I was never able to attend, as mum would always want me home at teatime to help with the domestic chores. Gradually I was to be kept at home more and more to help mum during the day, taking notes to the teacher. Not being very strong on arithmetic, I was to get further behind with this, and found it difficult to keep up with other subjects.

Once into the second year at school, all pupils in that year and upwards were taken on a school trip. Second years would have a trip in this country, and the next forms up would go abroad. When I heard we were due to go to Aysgarth in the Yorkshire Dales, I had to restrain myself from getting excited, as I knew mum would never tolerate this. It was a week in a youth hostel. We were all given forms to take home for parents to sign. I can remember quietly trying to persuade mum, only to be told, *'Stop pestering!'* I returned the form rejecting the offer. When the time came for the holiday, I counted each day my friends were away, and tried to visualise what Aysgarth Falls were like.

Long hot summer evenings were blocked out by my bedroom curtains. When mum was asked by my friends, *'Can Stephen play out tonight, Mrs. Lockwood?'* Already with my pyjamas on, I would listen to the usual answer from inside, *'No love, he's going to bed.'* Once upstairs, I could not resist the sunshine beating against the bedroom curtains as though it was objecting to the fact that they were drawn. Peeping between them, I would be spotted by Larry and his friends playing on the "Rec.". Mum soon became aware that they had noticed me, and would be up in a flash with a scolding.

A year or so on, mum decided to take a cleaning job, which was for the cousin of a lady she was friendly with down one of the streets. He was a widower, in his retirement years, by the name of Mr Thompson. After several months cleaning for him, he offered us all accommodation. Mum saw this as a means of escape from Bill's ties, and took up the offer.

Mr Thompson was a kind and generous man, concerned for us all, and very fond of mum. The house was dark and depressing, and definitely in need of a woman's touch. We moved in, leaving Spring Edge open views of the "Rec." in exchange for dark, contiguous houses within a few yards of ours. Back-to-back they were referred to. Edward Street, Walker Street, Holt Street, Nicholl Street, Scarborough Street, and so they went on. We were right in the middle. I was confused, rebelling in this tangled domestic scene and urban environment. Why couldn't mum live a life like my grandparents?

I was growing up now, and beginning to realise, within the next four years, that there was a world out there I could begin to explore myself. At school I began to daydream in the classroom. Where could I escape to? Where was the heart of Britain's countryside – that would feed me and allow me to grow unsuppressed? How did ordinary families live?

As I mentioned earlier, my Auntie Rita had a strong influence over her elder sister, my Auntie Margaret, as they were growing up. This was extended over my grandparents in their latter years. They had now lived in Lincolnshire around nine years and were approaching seventy. After their both being ill at times, Auntie Rita decided they were too far away in Lincolnshire for any member of the family to help, and so arranged for them to move back up to Yorkshire. Auntie Rita was living in a village called Barkisland, and knew a farmer close by who had his farm cottage to rent. Knowing grandad's love of the countryside and animals, she thought this would be a suitable home for them. So they moved back north and settled into their new home at "Far Barsey Farm Cottage". Needless to say, I welcomed this idea, and soon began my own bus journeys over to visit them.

My regular bus journeys over to the farm cottage resulted in my grandparents buying me a rabbit. He was white with a mink brown nose, ears and tail – a "Californian" by breeding – that I named Marcus. Grandad housed him in a hutch outside, next to the coalhouse, and I would put him inside in the winter. He was a challenge for me, growing into the biggest buck rabbit I have ever seen.

Over the years, my grandparents had taken less interest in Larry and were disappointed in his choice of company and the way he had begun to live his life. Not having a son of his own, and Larry being his first grandson, I think my grandfather was hoping they would be much closer. However, as Larry grew through his teens it was obvious he was inheriting his father's drink problem, along with keeping bad company, and eventually he left home after showing signs of bad temper.

Mum had hoped, as he left school, that he would become – as she expected – the man of the house; that he would bring in a wage to help support her and the home. She was angry that this did not happen, and began to tell everyone how I was not like Larry, and would not leave home, but would stay and look after her. I was still very quiet and shy and accepted this was what maybe would happen, though deep in my mind I had begun to imagine what life could really be like.

Mum's relationship with Larry's teenage friend Desmond

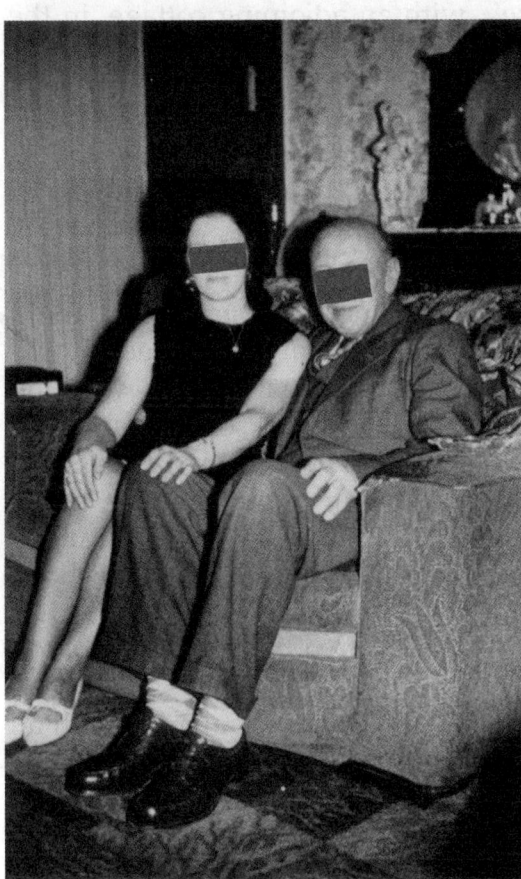

had taken somewhat of a back seat since her move into Edward Street, as she was now valuing Mr Thompson's relationship I know Mr Thompson had asked mum to sleep with him, but she refused, and we all had our own bedrooms. One morning, about nine months after moving in, mum went into Mr Thompson's bedroom to wake him for work, as she always did. As there was no response, she realised he had

Mum and
Mr Thompson.

passed away in his sleep during the night. I recall her being very saddened, and as she called for his cousin, who lived in a house across the road, we were all being prepared for school amongst the commotion.

Mr Thompson had one son, but in his will had left mum the sum of £600, along with a new three-piece suite he had bought and other furnishings. It was 1965 when Mr Thompson died.

Somehow, eventually, probably with some persuasion from myself, mum seemed to recognise my longing for the country, and after suggesting to Keith, Darren and me that we might live there, an overwhelming response from us all in favour led her to purchase a large detached house, "Well Ings House", with an adjoining cottage, in the village of Stainland. Mum took us to look at the house, which the landlord showed us, explaining that there were also several acres of allotments, from which he drew rents, that he would like to sell along with the house. Mum was not interested, and not business minded to see what their long-term investment might be, but did agree to rent one allotment for me to keep chickens.

In 1966 we moved into our new home, which mum purchased for the sum of £400, cottage included. I was now twelve years old, and my imagination was working overtime. Keith had now changed special schools, and was picked up by coach every morning to travel to Hartshead Moor, near Cleckheaton. Darren started at Bowling Green Junior School in the village, and a bus pass was arranged so that I could continue at Haugh Shaw Secondary School. My grandparents bought me a brand-new leather satchel, which I carried with pride on my two bus journeys to and from school.

When grandad heard of my allotment, he arrived with all the help and advice that a young boy could wish for when starting a new hobby. With such enthusiasm for outdoor life, even at this age, it seemed his artificial leg was never given a thought as he reached the top of the ladder to

This is Well-Ings House which Mum purchased in 1966 after the death of Mr Thompson.

Haugh Shaw Secondary School 1968. Me, far left, second row back from front.

hand me the clout heads, whilst instructing me where to put them into the new roll of tarpaulin we had just laid on the hen house roof.

Grandad told my uncle George, who had his own livestock in some buildings at Norland a few miles away, of my new venture. At Norland he was allowed to keep cows, pigs and hens and to grow vegetables, in return for looking after an old lady by the name of Mrs Hall, who owned the buildings and land adjacent to her home. Shortly after, Uncle George arrived with one broody bantam hen and a beautifully coloured bantam cockerel. I couldn't believe my eyes. When he opened a box containing one dozen large, rich brown mirran hen eggs, I listened eagerly as he told me that, by placing them under the broody bantam, I would have my own mirran chickens in three weeks' time.

Making friends with a farmer and his grandsons in the village, all my spare time was spent haymaking, milking cows, and swapping hens from my allotment. I was soon to realise that to stock and maintain my allotment as I wanted to was going to cost money, and I wasn't frightened of working to earn some. Some of my friends had newspaper rounds, and the newsagents across from our house were offering attractive wages – fifty pence a week. I knew one paper round was not very popular with the other boys because the deliveries were too spread out, but this suited me fine, as the route took me two miles through country in the direction of Auntie Rita and Uncle George's home at Barkisland. As soon as the round became vacant I applied. Being a few months short of my thirteenth birthday, I was told I was not old enough though, with a lot of persuasion, Mr and Mrs Canning, the newsagents, were willing to take the risk and set me on; I learnt the round within a week. Straight after school I would collect my paper bag, challenging myself to better the record time for my previous deliveries. Fridays were always much slower, as they were "collecting nights". As the customers settled their accounts, I would be offered sweets, drinks and tips, which were all gratefully received. On occasions, when I reached my last delivery, which was in the bottom of the valley, I would continue up the road for about three quarters of a mile to visit my Auntie and Uncle and Cousin Robert, who was still at school and hoping to become a joiner. They would be having tea, and always insisted I joined them. I would take the same route back home, passing Maude's woollen mill in the valley bottom, where Auntie Rita worked as a weaver. When there were times I needed to be home early, the workers' coach driver allowed me a lift back up to the village.

My stock at the allotment grew to over one hundred chickens and ducks, one cat, two ferrets and a very faithful terrier dog named Rex, who became a constant companion and a first-class rabbit-hole finder.

By the age of fourteen, I had two permanent paper rounds, and would stand in on a third when one boy was on his holidays. In between, I would deliver duck eggs in the village from my own ducks, though there were lots of hungry mouths at home to consume all the hen eggs.

All this work made for good pocket money and an opportunity to start and save. However, this was not to be, there were bills to be paid in the home and now I was the eldest at home, and mum's expectations of my financing the home were becoming harder for me to bear. Larry had left home when of working age without supporting us, and I could see mum was beginning to lean heavily on me already. This made for constant arguments, along with her telling me I was not doing my share of domestic chores.

By now Larry's friend, Desmond, was back on the scene, and their relationship strong enough for mum to allow him to live with us. She encouraged him to play a father role over me, which may have worked had I been much younger, but now that I was almost ready for leaving school, I resented this, and an unsettled atmosphere in the home reared its ugly head once again.

Spending more and more time on the farm, with long, hot summer days in the hay field until eleven o'clock in the evening, the farmer would treat us all to a fish and chip supper and as much "pop" as we could drink from a crate which was a permanent supply in the farmhouse kitchen. I became so absorbed in life there, both as a matter of interest and escape, that I found myself milking the cows regularly by myself. There would be frequent visits from Keith, with messages from mum to tell me to come home immediately. I would go red with embarrassment as the farmer and my friends listened, knowing they were aware of my mum's growing reputation for her hot temper.

My hen house at the allotment offered sanctuary for me where, after feeding time, when not working on the farm, I would shut the hens in one half and sit by the corn bins watching them preening as they settled down to roost for the evening. I felt secure and peaceful with the door locked, dreaming and scheming what I would do when I left home. As darkness fell, the thought of going home became harder, knowing there would be trouble waiting in one form or another. It was at this point I felt I really wanted to know God, and prayed with all my heart for him to make me strong. None of my family, including my grandparents, were strict church people, though they did believe, but only attended christenings, weddings and funerals. This never bothered me as my grandparents were good-living people, and never meant anyone harm.

In our home there were times of not exactly peace, but easier times, when mum would teach us right from wrong, and say to us how God was good and would look after us when things were hard. This was comforting when I was younger but as I grew older I found it confusing, as I would find she would use the words 'God is good' to whichever one of us she was on bad terms with, leaving us with a feeling of total guilt and as though God would punish us for her hard times.

Whether times were hard or easier, mum would always have us spotlessly clean and well clothed. She always firmly believed cleanliness was next to godliness. There were lean times, when coming home from school, after asking what was for tea, we would be told, *'Bread and pull it'*. Or, if she was in a bad mood, we would be told to get something from the corner shop. In her better moods, I recall a welcome smell of braised liver and sausage with onions, accompanied with mashed potatoes and peas. This was a regular dish. She was a good baker and, when in the right frame of mind, could turn out cakes by the half dozen. The general scene, though, was erratic, and we never knew what was happening from one day to another. Planning was non-existent, and I feel she could only cope with her situation by taking one day at a time, which was difficult for me to understand at that age. Things always seemed much more organised at my grandparents' home and, when I was not at Cousin Robert's, telling him of my plans to be a farmer, I would be at their farm cottage tending to my rabbit, chopping wood, filling their coal buckets, or helping in whatever way I could.

"Far Barsey Cottage" heralded a period of support; support of my interests in life from my grandparents, who were now always there, and so in turn I could discuss flora and fauna easily. Looking back now, I realise I was using my grandparents as though they were my own parents, and would take great heed of whatever they said or advised – grandad's word was gospel. Although they were of senior years, their patience for me never ran short.

As I spent all my school holidays with them, I got to know the farmer from whom they rented the cottage, and would have conversation with him in the mistal at milking time. A lady in her fifties by the name of Ethel, who came to the farm as a "land girl" during the war, would let me turn the milk bottles for her whilst she operated the bottle-washing machine. She was a lady of few words, wearing a woolly bonnet winter and summer alike, and permanently holding a cigarette in her mouth in a way that looked to me as though she had forgotten it was there. The dairy, where the bottle washing took place, would be like a Turkish bath as it filled with steam. Again, I would challenge myself as I did on the paper round; this time to see how fast I could turn the bottles in the crates. As I departed, without Ethel exchanging more than half a dozen words, I knew she had enjoyed my company and looked forward to me helping her again the next day.

Inside, my grandparents would have tea ready, with that distinctive smell coming through the cottage door into the farmyard. As usual, I was encouraged to pick the bones and mop up my gravy with a slice of bread – that was where all the goodness was grandad would say and, of course, he was right. Then, after a few house chores, I would join them in watching television. As grandad approached the sideboard drawer, I was given strict instructions by Nan to be quiet, as this was a sign that the football results were being given and he was collecting his glasses and pen to mark his coupon. The evening finished with "Match of the Day", as they were both keen football supporters. This interest was heightened by watching his nephew, Ray Clemence, who played goalkeeper for Liverpool. After the news I would collect my nightshirt from the drawer, which was actually grandad's day shirt, a striped, collarless garment that came below my knees. The toilet was outside, at the bottom of the farmyard, and so my last call of nature would be to an enamel bucket kept in the kitchen, which also accommodated their "g'sunder" contents, which I willingly emptied daily. Whilst they placed the fireguard round the fire, I would watch the last of the glow die away as they covered me over with blankets on the sofa to the smell of mothballs from the nightshirt. Hearing grandad's artificial leg squeak its way upstairs to their bedroom, I would close my eyes in gratitude for what the day had offered me – a contented mind.

The happy memories of "Far Barsey Cottage" are many;

walking to the top of the farm lane with Nan to meet the travelling library, and helping her choose a book; playing on the farm with my cousin when he would visit; helping grandad to row the hayfields by hand on long, hot summer evenings; and bringing the cows up from the valley bottom at milking time. Amongst these were two things that had a flavour of humour, if not to me and my grandad at the time, then certainly to the rest of the family.

Grandad, being a very true example of a Yorkshireman, decided one day that our visit to the barber, with the price of a haircut being raised to 2/6d, and bus fares taken into account, was proving too expensive, and decided to send for a pair of his own hair shears with the coupons he had saved from Nan's cigarettes; she was quite a heavy smoker. When the shears arrived, my auntie heard of his intentions and told him not to practise on my hair. However, Auntie Rita's influence did not work on that occasion, and I was put on a buffet and literally sheared. What bit of hair remained was in the shape of a basin. As I was almost reduced to tears, they bought me a school cap that I wore permanently on the farm until I returned to school but, of course, grandad was right, and I would not have had it any other way.

Then there was the time he was influenced by "Daz". The farmer bred his own shire horses which, when they heard their buckets of bran rattle at feeding time, would come thundering across the field, making the ground tremble at your feet. At show times he would lead them into the farmyard and tie them to the wall outside the cottage. He would then proceed to wash each of the great white fetlocks by standing them in a bucket of water to which he added "Daz" soap powder. This produced the most beautiful soft, white finish to the hair as it hung gracefully over their hooves. Nan, grandad and I would stand and watch with great admiration, as those magnificent animals were so willing to co-operate.

On one of my daily visits between my holiday stays,

mum went with me to see my grandparents and found it unusual that the door was closed. When Nan answered the door, she said, with some concern, yet with a hint of serves him right, silly old fool – *'Come and look what your dad's done, Laura!'* As we entered the kitchen, grandad's face was unrecognisable. Because grandad's hair was pure white, he thought he would try the same shampoo as the shire horses, only to find that his skin was not quite as tough as theirs, which resulted in his bloodstream being poisoned and his face swelling and turning bright red all over, looking as though he had been burnt in a fire. Mum was horrified, and I can remember being very upset, though in a couple of weeks his complexion had returned to normal. It took a long time for him to live that story down but grandad was a great one for pulling people's legs and took it all in good part.

This period of my life also helped me with my schooling. One summer holiday our Science teacher gave us a list of topics to choose from; we had to write four thousand words on a topic of our choice. Mine was "Animals and their Habitats". I spent the whole six weeks' holiday at my grandparents, studying in front of their well-tended coal fire with nature books that grandad had built into volumes, and had not let anyone else read. I felt so privileged, and ultimately greatly rewarded, as my topic took first prize in the class. This entitled me to a book voucher, which I exchanged for the most beautifully illustrated book entitled, "Lakeland in Colour", a place it was my ambition to visit.

Chapter Five

The day finally came when I had to leave school. Mum knew how strongly I felt about wanting to become a farmer, and was not at all happy, as she knew it was very poor wages for long hours, which did not worry me but I knew that she knew this would not support the home. The area was not a good farming area, and those farms like and including the one on which I helped in the village were antiquated in their methods, and could only really support themselves adequately.

I left school with no qualifications and people in my position were doomed for one type of work – the mill. The thought sent shivers down my spine. *'It's good money and it's time you brought some wage home here! I've brought you up on next to nothing all these years!'* mum would declare.

I knew if I was to stand my ground on this issue I would have to leave home, as good farming prospects were in other parts of the country. Mum knew of my thoughts and began to turn bitter towards me. Was she right? Had I a duty to stay and support the home? Above all, I did not want to leave with such bitterness from mum. Yes, I could understand she had lived through bad times with us and supported us, but did this mean my future had to be sacrificed? I could not help feeling resentment towards her, as I was faced with a decision I would not have had to make had we had a father. I wanted to leave home with pride and encouragement of the career I wanted to pursue.

Plans had been made deep within my heart, how I would

go away and earn good wages at a job I would enjoy, to be able to return and finance mum to allow her a comfortable living. However, with threats that she would not recognise me again if I left home, I did not feel strong enough against her wishes, and in the end compromised by taking a job in a chicken factory just outside the village, with a weekly wage of £12.00.

As the summer went on, this proved unbearable for me, working indoors with battery hens I found monotonous. Fortunately, mum was not too keen on the outcome either, as I had to bath every night due to carrying pests on me, transmitted from the chickens, which made for more housework for mum. Eventually, a local farmer with a good-sized milk round offered me a job, which I took, along with a drop in wages to £7.50 a week. The situation was not ideal, and after mum speaking to a joiner in the village, who was giving up his apprenticeship to work in the mill for more wages, she asked him to make enquiries for work for me. Jobs were easy to come by in the mill in those days, and interviews weren't needed. He soon returned saying there was work for me and I could start straight away on a wage of £12.00 a week. Mum had won, and what's more, there was overtime to be had, which I was encouraged to take – bringing my wage up to £14.00 a week. This allowed me to go on "board", which again mum was not happy about, as she thought I should contribute my whole wage to the home, making for more bad feelings.

In 1971, the family was yet to increase again. Mum suffered long periods of sickness whilst carrying Desmond's baby, which she didn't take lightly as she was always strong in herself and extremely active where housework was concerned. We were all to pay the price during those nine months, being at her beck and call. Desmond, however, was very caring, and I must say, obedient to mum's requirements. My two younger brothers and sister were placed in foster care during this time.

On the 12th May 1971 mum gave birth to a baby girl.

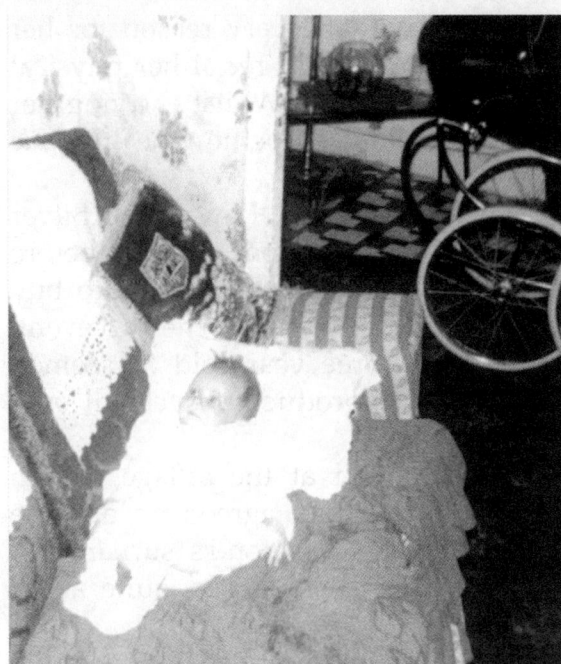

New born baby
Sandra with silver
cross pram Well-Ings
House 1971.

This is Mum proudly
hanging out her daily
wash in the garden at
Well-Ings House. This
was the first garden I
made at 12 years old.

53

Mum would now tell us this was the very reason for her having a difficult pregnancy, and would recall her physical and mental state whilst carrying Paula. Whilst carrying her sons, on the other hand, she would tell us how healthy she had been.

I recall a beautiful navy blue, Rolls Royce-type Silver Cross pram standing in the dining room months before the baby was due. A special effort had been made to buy this brand-new pram and its accessories for the big event. After all, mum was now forty-three years old. It seemed as though she was starting her reproductive cycle all over again.

Soon a christening was arranged at the village church in Stainland. Mum and Desmond had agreed on a name – Sandra – who was also to take Desmond's surname. A tiny being with lots of dark hair, she caused quite a stir with all the attention.

The bond between mum and Desmond was now quite strong, though not strong enough for marriage. I was finding it increasingly difficult to get any support for my interest in farming. Mum now had a new baby, and the feeling was that I was in Desmond's way. I realised my main reason for living at home was to bring in some wages.

One day there was a furious argument, and I remember mum asking Desmond to behave like a father to me and to show his authority. I can't remember what I must have done or said, but whatever it was resulted in Sandra's father holding me down on the floor and telling me he was the boss in the house and I would have to abide by him, as this was mum's wish.

When he released me, I walked out of the house with that incident giving me a bitter memory of the pain I was feeling for the want of love and just to be needed by a family, my own family. I walked and prayed for miles over fields and footpaths, eventually arriving at my auntie and uncle's in the next village. Their surprise on my arrival

Walter and Gladys Clemence on their Golden Wedding Day.

Celebrations for former licensee

MR AND MRS WALTER CLEMENCE, of Far Barsey Farm Cottage, Barkisland, will celebrate their golden wedding tomorrow.

They were married at Halifax Register Office and have three daughters, eleven grandchildren and three great-grandchildren.

Mr Clemence (75), born at Norwich, came to Halifax with his parents when he was eight. His first job was as a pony and cart driver for the Economic Stores, Halifax, at a wage of 12s a week

Afterwards, he worked for a time at the former Whitley's Hanson Lane Mills, as a reeler, then, for some 26 years, he was employed by Riley Bros (Hx.) Ltd, manufacturing confectioners, as a case maker at their Kingston Mills.

For nine years he was licensee of the Waggoners' Rest Inn at Stocks Lane, Luddenden.

Following his retirement, in 1958, he and his wife went to live at Spilsby, near Skegness (Lincs), near Mr Clemence's brother, before coming to live at Barkisland.

Mr Clemence volunteered for service in World War One and saw four years' service, chiefly in France, as a driver and gunner in the Royal Field Artillery.

He was wounded and lost a leg at a spot between Ypres and Passchendaele, in Belgium.

He is a former member of Halifax and District Branch of the British Limbless Ex-Servicemen's Association.

His nephew, Raymond Clemence, is Liverpool FC's first team goalkeeper.

Varied career

Mrs Clemence, formerly Miss Gladys Lord, was born in Birks Hall Terrace, Pellon Lane, Halifax, and used to be a regular attender at the Wall Nook Methodist Chapel, Barkisland.

She, too, has had a varied career, having worked in an hotel at Spilsby, and also at one time for 22 years at the former Luddenden Spinning Company's mill.

They are holding a family gathering at Spring Rock Inn, Barkisland, on Saturday, and a dinner in the evening.

My grandparents celebrated their golden wedding while we lived at Well-Ings House 1971.

56

This is Mum with Aunty Betty her friend. Taken at Well-Ings House shortly after the Birth of Sandra.

soon turned to realisation of why I was there, as I choked, holding back the tears whilst trying to explain my misery at home. I was also finding things difficult with Darren. He and Keith being of a similar age, and Keith having the soft nature he had, Darren would see me as an intruder and encourage Keith not to spend time with me.

I had only been at my auntie and uncle's about one hour when a knock came at the door. It was Keith, telling Auntie Rita mum had sent him over in a taxi with my bags, which she had packed, and I had not to return home again. It was

This is Grandad age 18 in his army uniform 1914.

Me at my bedroom window where I took the photo of Mum in the garden on page 53. Well-Ings House 1971. Age 17.

July 1971. After Keith had left, I remember crying aloud and being consoled by my auntie and uncle and cousin Robert. I shall never forget that feeling till the day I die.

Keith was a friendly soul and of an impressionable nature, and would talk to or do anything for anyone, and it hurt me so much to think he had been chosen to do this task. I often longed to try and explain to him how to take care of himself but did not want to confuse him, and although he was being dominated by Darren, I knew he needed him and mum more than I did.

In July 1971 I was 17 years old, healthy and full of outdoor life and was useful labour for any farmer. Although Auntie Rita and Uncle George understood my difficulties and realised my ambition for farming, they knew they were unable to let me stay with them for very long without my earning my keep. They asked me if I would agree to living down in Somerset with farming friends of Auntie Margaret and Uncle John so that I would be able to get some farming experience whilst leaving my home troubles behind, and hopefully, starting a new life. This was a big step; I had never been away from home before, and was torn between the relish of adventure and prospects of losing my friends and relationship with Yorkshire, which I loved so dearly.

I realised I wasn't in a position to refuse, and whilst arrangements were being made for my work and accommodation in Somerset, Auntie Rita got me a job at the mill in the valley, where she worked as a weaver.

At the mill where I was currently working in the next valley, I had befriended a lady by the name of Margaret. Margaret knew I wasn't mill material, and I found it difficult to stand up to the antics of the others. During my lunch hours, I would escape up the valley and settle down in a meadow with my packed lunch to watch nature in the heat of the summer, whilst at the same time listening to the huge machines in the distance, working their way through the moors to build the M62 Pennine Motorway. Eventually, on these lunchtime visits, I was able to watch them building a bridge across the Scammonden Valley, which was at that time to be the longest, single span bridge in Europe. The motorway was to change those moors for ever, but the valley and the mill still remain unspoilt.

Margaret and I said our goodbyes, and I started work at Bower's Mill, which was in walking distance from my auntie and uncle's house at Barkisland. My duty was as "weft boy" in the weaving shed, to supply the weft to the weavers, who would tend proudly to their Dobcross looms with their picking sticks, sending the weft to and fro on a shuttle that seemed to me to be travelling at the speed of a bullet. On entering the weaving shed, after clocking on in the morning, there would be a surge of people rushing to see who could get their loom into action first, as they were on "piece work". As the first loom would start to clatter, so would the second, and another, and another, and so on, until, within ten minutes, the whole shed would vibrate to the deafening sound of dozens of looms turning out their produce.

The day finally came some weeks later when I received news that I could book my coach ticket to travel down to Somerset where my Cousin Andy, who was Auntie Margaret and Uncle John's eldest son, had found me a job as a farm labourer in the village of Othery where they lived. I was to live with Andy's wife's mother, who had a large family by her late husband, all of whom contributed to the farm work.

Whilst I was staying with Auntie Rita and Uncle George, they had told me that I was unable to keep my ferrets and would also have to find a new home for my dog, Rex, whom I loved dearly and knew was my only true friend. I soon found a buyer for my ferrets but, holding back day after day, I couldn't bring myself to part with Rex. Eventually, they told me I should try the R.S.P.C.A., as they would probably find him a home, and so, with a couple of days to go before my departure, I took Rex to the R.S.P.C.A. in Halifax, which was down in the old Woolshops in those days, just below the abattoir. A tall, well-built man, with a light voice, took details in a very offhand manner, as apparently he was inundated with homeless cats and dogs. As I closed the door to leave, I turned back and dared to ask him, *'Will he get a home alright?'* *'I wouldn't think so,'* the man replied callously. *'Seventy per cent of them have to be put down if we haven't found a home within five days; we have more than we can cope with.'* As I left the building, clutching Rex's collar and lead, I felt my heart break as the lump in my throat was followed by floods of tears while I walked back up through the town, aware I was being noticed.

The coach journey down to Othery was a long one. I remember it with mixed feelings. Changing at Cheltenham, the journey was eleven hours in all.

I was greeted at Bridgewater by my auntie and uncle, who chauffeured me to their home in their Ford Consul car. Everyone made me welcome and my lodgings were comfortable. I made lots of friends, but I had been warned that my boss at the farm wasn't an easy taskmaster. He turned out to live up to his reputation; he made me shiver in my boots. The work itself, though hard, I enjoyed. Farming was very different down there to what I had been used to back home. It was on a much larger scale, with arable included. Milking was done outside, miles away from the farm where the cows were grazing, in what was called a "milking bale". This was a portable tin shed, which would be towed from field to field and had its own engine, which we would start by cranking.

I worked hard, and saved money for the first time in my life. I was allowed to keep my own eleven piglets on the farm, which I reared and sold at Taunton cattle market for £411.00 which, after paying back the farmer for their keep, made me a profit of about 50%. There was a good social life, in which I was included – taking part in skittle nights and other outings.

Though everyone, except my boss, was trying very hard to make me feel at home, I knew that my lodgings were

Keith with Rex winter in the garden Well-Ings House 1970.

Rex would walk the valleys with me to find rabbit holes. Scammonden 1970.

Me with Rupert my blonde ferret and Rex. Well-Ings House 1970.

only temporary and I would have to find a home of my own in time. Somerset wasn't the place where I wanted to live permanently. Yorkshire was my home, and my heart began to yearn for the feel of the hills, the stone and the stories my grandad had told me of the "Yorkshire Dales", a place I was determined to share my life with.

Then there was mum. She had written to me on a couple of occasions during the ten months I lived there. Although I had not spoken about her letters to my relatives, they knew I had received them and would question me as to what mum had said. They knew I was upset by some of the contents, and told me I would be a fool to consider going back home. The contents of the letters were a mixture of telling me what she had done for me all her life and that she did not deserve me treating her in this way, which was said with so much bitterness yet, at the same time, suggesting she and the rest of the family were missing me. This began to instil in me such a feeling of guilt that I felt it difficult to cope with. In the years ahead, I was to learn that I would receive such letters whenever I went away from home.

With the force and influence of my relatives in Somerset for me to stay, I began to feel more and more that I was doing something wrong. I felt I was at the heart of a family feud, unable to express my own feelings, which were becoming more and more confused. Eventually, one evening after work, I went into the village kiosk and telephoned mum. I was pleasantly surprised to hear her voice, in which I seemed to detect a hint of caring. As she asked me about my work I broke down, knowing I dreaded every minute of my boss's presence. Mum suggested I paid her a visit, and that if I was unhappy, I should stay back up in Yorkshire, as there was a place for me at home. I took the bait.

When I informed my auntie and uncle I wished to pay mum a visit, they were extremely angry. They told me my life would not work out as I wanted it to if I kept contacting her, but the decision was mine and I would lose all support from them if I did. I returned to my lodgings upset but decided in my mind I had a journey to make; and I felt it would be one way.

The next day, I very nervously handed my notice in to my employer, upon which I received lots of personal abuse about my mother, as he told me how he had been informed about her by my relatives. This made me realise how he had been exploiting my situation in terms of hard labour.

I had not dared mention my arrangements to my Cousin Andy, as I knew he would not approve, having found me the job and all. Knowing he would eventually find out from a member of the family when he returned from a journey he had taken involving cattle, I drew my savings of a few hundred pounds out of the Post Office and booked a taxi for 4.00 a.m. the next morning so that I would not have to confront him. With some of the money, I bought a large bouquet of flowers for Mrs Pimm, my landlady, Andy's mother-in-law, who had been very kind to me. With it I left a letter of thanks addressed to Andy, apologising for all the inconvenience I had caused.

As I lay in bed that night I could not sleep, frightened of Andy finding me before my taxi arrived at 4.00 a.m. At 1.00 a.m. I heard raised voices downstairs; within seconds Andy came upstairs. As I was trying to rouse myself, he burst into the bedroom and began to shake me furiously, scolding me for all the inconvenience and time wasted on his part. He told me he never wanted to see me again. After he left I never slept, but cried with the thought that I had upset someone, as this was the last thing in my life I wanted to do.

Four o'clock came, and as I walked up the road, leaving the sleepy farm buildings behind, my two suitcases in hand, I prayed I could pass my auntie and uncle's house in the village without anyone else seeing me. Three miles up the road my taxi approached, and once at the train station I knew I was homeward bound. The strange thing is, that not until I find myself writing this now, do I realise that that moment as the train pulled out of the station was a mirrored experience of when the train pulled out of Doncaster station back in 1962, with mum and her brood fleeing from Billy, her second husband.

Though my departure was not a pleasant one, as I sat on the train travelling north I looked at myself objectively. Always aware of my choice of clothes, I admired my dark brown corduroy jacket, which I had only worn a few times, along with my clean shirt, fawn corduroy trousers and suede "sneakers". Coyly, I glanced at my reflection in the window as we passed through a tunnel, but then before it disappeared, with a more positive look at myself, I realised I had actually made a decision in life for myself; probably upsetting quite a few people. I was also beginning to realise that it was so easy to upset people in this life, and having a mother with such a volatile nature made me very sensitive to this, making it difficult for me to socialise and enter into new company.

Chapter Six

My attempt to continue writing this book between January 1994 and March 1994 was brief but a detailed account of a very difficult and stressful time. Some ten years after I first began, I am able to continue writing.

When setting out to write this book in 1992 in my Florist shop in Hebden Bridge, I knew I was going to find the time factor a challenge in terms of completing it; though I could not envisage what life itself would burden me with in the few years ahead.

It is now ten years on – Sunday, 24th March 2002. I am 47 years old, with a son of my own who will be having his 15th birthday next month. The force within me to continue writing is no less than when I mentioned it at the beginning of my book. So, thank you for staying with me as I continue to unfold the years after my train journey back from Somerset in the summer of 1972.

Mum had made every effort to welcome me back home and, as always, however much emotional hurt was caused to each other, as a mother she was always totally forgiving, but the experience she put me through by forcing me to leave home had left its mark on me.

We had agreed in our last telephone conversation whilst I was in Somerset that, if I came home, it would only be temporary until I found some lodgings. I couldn't bear the hurt of being rejected again, and realised that part of the process of becoming an adult was that I was now able to make a decision about my own future. Things were good now, and however severely our relationship had been damaged, a bond seemed to form, almost as though mum could accept my living away again, as long as it wasn't with any of her sister's family.

Mum's new baby girl was now a year old and creating lots of attention. It was good to be back. I had experienced a terrible sense of loss of family and of my beloved Yorkshire moors, hills and dales.

Eventually, after only a few weeks working on the village farm, where I had spent many previous years, they offered me a "live-in" position as a farm labourer. Both mum and I knew it would only be temporary, but I worked very hard and enjoyed life for what it was at the time.

It had been a hot summer and I would call down from the farm some evenings to see mum and my brothers and sisters. One day, in September, I recall mum saying to me, *'I want you to be home here for eight o'clock as I have a surprise for you.'* I could tell she was very pleased with herself, which made me feel good. I remember coming home that late summer evening, making sure I was on time, as instructed. When I asked everyone what was happening, no one would tell me. Only at twenty minutes past eight, when a knock came at the door, did mum say to me, *'You'd better come, I think this is for you.'*

A strongly-built man, with an outdoor complexion, stood at the door. As mum ushered me to go with him, I saw across the road was parked a pale green Austin 1100 car, with "JACKSON SCHOOL OF MOTORING" mounted on the top. My breath was taken away; as I turned back to face mum as she stood at the door, I could see her face full of pride. I was also filled with pride, as I realised the dedication mum had shown towards me as one of her children through this gesture. She had once, some years ago, had the opportunity to learn to drive herself, and I remember seeing her arrive home, learning to drive a lovely well-cared-for Morris Minor but, although mum would say she never really had the nerve to continue, I have always felt that the real truth was that she was so committed to her children that she didn't have the time or the money to continue whilst bringing us up. This was one of many sacrifices she made for us.

I will never forget her proud smile as she waved me off on that first of seven driving lessons, which she paid for, continuing from 19th September 1972 to 31st October 1972. I can remember her constantly saying to me *'Don't worry about your test, you'll pass first time.'* Needless to say, I was so proud when I returned from my test to be able to tell her that I had passed.

Ellistone's Farm, where I worked in the village, was run by a family of cattle dealers. Four brothers by the name of Crowther worked the farm for their grandfather and grandmother Thornton, who owned it, though by now they were well in their eighties. Those years spent with them as a schoolboy, before going to Somerset, were boundless. I was allowed to try anything and everything on the farm: milking cows, riding horses, driving vehicles. I had built so much confidence in myself driving the farm Land Rover and other vehicles, that when it came to my driving lessons in the car, it was second nature to me, but now mum had opened up a whole new world for me.

Shortly after passing my driving test mum had put the family home up for sale. It was a sad time for me; I don't know how mum felt at the time but "Well Ings House" was one house we had spent the longest time in (six years), and so there were lots of memories. The winds of change were blowing, and maybe mum felt that because I had left home, there was now no need for such a large house in the country with an allotment. By this time her relationship with Sandra's father was over. Sandra was now two years old and mum and the rest of the family moved to a town house in a street in Sowerby Bridge, which was nearer to Halifax. Country life suits me, but mum feels happier closer to towns. I was, and still am, very grateful for those six years she gave to us in the country.

Mum was so impatient for me to get on the road with my

own vehicle now, and had contacted one of her old flames, Teddy Pickles. He was a mechanic and mum bought me a secondhand Cortina. I could not have saved quickly enough myself to buy a car so soon. Although I appreciated it at the time, it is not until now, looking back, that I realise how very lucky I was.

The hand-painted, blue and cream car was delivered to mum's house and I was handed the keys. My dream could now come true. After years as a schoolboy listening passionately to my grandad telling me about the Yorkshire Dales, I could now explore them. He told me how it was better farming country than around Halifax. Mum knew this was my chosen route and was pleased to let me spread my wings.

I immediately began buying the newspaper for the Dales, scouring it for dairy farm vacancies, and after arranging an interview, one clear, crisp morning, as proud as Punch, I drove up to Gargrave, a small village five miles north of Skipton, in my new, secondhand car, and wearing a cream cable-knit winter jumper.

The interview was successful, and in January 1973 I said my goodbyes to Ellistone's Farm and friends I had made in Stainland village. I reassured mum that I would keep in touch and visit regularly. Gargrave was not too far away, which made me feel easy about being able to come home and visit.

I moved into Raybridge Farm with Mr and Mrs Green on Sunday, 21st January 1973, to start work on the Monday. They were a kind couple, and made me feel very welcome. I was to share a room with a Lancashire lad of similar age called Brian, who was studying at college. We shared duties and became good friends throughout our working time at Raybridge Farm.

My life had truly opened up. It was idyllic. Long, hot summer days, hard work on the farm, social evenings at the Country Youth Club, and my own car to visit home on my weekend off, every three weeks.

My friend Brian, on left, and me with Brian's first car, a Ford Anglia. We both lived in and worked together at Raybridge Farm Gargrave 1973–1974.

Brian and me returning from hand scything thistles in the meadows at Raybridge Farm Gargrave 1973–1974.

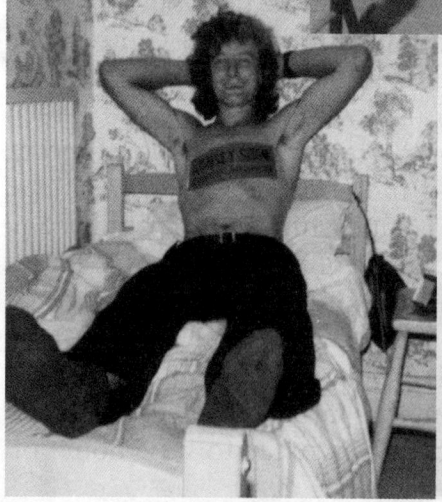

Myself. After a night out at the local rugby club Brian would be a little worse for wear. We would both find it difficult to get to sleep on the long hot summer evenings, resulting in playing pranks on each other. Raybridge Farm Gargrave 1973–1974.

I was becoming very fit, competing with Brian at certain tasks on the farm. Mr Green had taken notice of how I had been very keen to run in the hayfields stacking bales, rounding cows up and choosing to run whenever it was possible instead of using the tractor. He told me about a race that was held in the village every August, called a "Fell Race". I had never heard of this sport before, and decided to enter.

Somewhat hesitant on the day, and quite shy in new company, I prepared myself for the race at Gargrave Agricultural Show. The route went through fields and up Sharpaw Fell, which stood behind Raybridge Farm. I had practised running up in the evenings during the hay season, but now this was the big day. Twenty or so healthy looking athletes from various parts of the Dales and Lake District warmed up and chatted to me with some inquisitiveness as a new runner. I had a gut feeling I belonged with this lot.

The gun went off, and within half an hour we had run to the top of Sharpaw and back. There were eight prizes of small token sums of money, and I finished eighth. I was elated. They accepted me as a fell runner and my whole world changed.

Chapter Seven

On Saturday, 18th August 1973 I was to meet someone who was to become a life-long friend.

Once all the runners had returned to the show field, after the Fell Race at Gargrave, and we had collected our prizes, there was lots of camaraderie. Two runners showed particular interest in me; both were well known runners and lived in the Lake District. The winner of the race was a lean man, several years older than me, by the name of Fred Reeves, who ran with ease and a comfortable style. He was impressed by my first performance and encouraged me to keep contact, and to continue fell running. Little did I know that I was to spend many years under his wing, training and running alongside him. Whilst chatting, he became aware I was a herdsman, and introduced me to another runner of the same occupation, by the name of Tony Nicholson.

It is now thirty years ago, during which time Tony and I have remained good friends.

Before we all left the show field, Tony enthused about his life in "The Lakes", and how he was enjoying his running, both on the track and fell. He gave me his address and invited me up, suggesting he could find me a herdsman's job with one of his friends. Sometimes people say these kinds of things but never manage to keep contact for whatever reason. How serious Tony was about his offer at the time I'm not sure, but now, ever adventurous, I took him up on it, whilst keeping contact through running during the rest of that year. Tony arranged an interview for me with his farming friends.

I drove up one ice cold winter's day, with clear blue sky and fells and mountains capped with snow. I was ecstatic. Tony was right; the scenery was beautiful. Arriving at his small, isolated bungalow between Penrith and Keswick, I breathed as deep as I could, filling my lungs with this elixir, whilst feeling the blood rushing through my veins. All I wanted to do was run up those mountains.

Tony's mum greeted me at the door, and Tony followed shortly after. It was good to see each other, and we had lots to talk about as Tony took me to meet his friends for an informal interview.

Hesket Farm was in a beautiful setting, nestling between the fells on the outskirts of a small village called Dacre. John and Margaret were very welcoming. I had never been this far north before, and found everyone very warm and friendly. Their jovial Cumbrian banter appealed to me. It was a larger, mixed farm compared with where I was at the time, and had eighty milkers with followers, several sucklers and a few hundred sheep.

I accepted the position as herdsman, and moved up to "live in" at Hesket Farm on Monday, 15th April 1974.

The work rota was the same as that of Raybridge Farm – working three weeks, and then having a full weekend off. I always drove home on my weekends off, usually incorporating a fell race on the way. My circle of friends was increasing, mostly on the fell running scene, but Tony and Fred remained my main influence.

I was now approaching my 21st birthday and had been giving my future some thought – wondering how I was going to make a living for the rest of my life. Work was still stable in most areas in those days, but I had realised I would never be able to afford to buy a piece of machinery, let alone run my own farm. I was feeling ambitious and restless towards my work, and knew I had reached a crossroads in my life. Both Fred and Tony were very supportive in listening and helping me to work my way through things. Following lots of discussions, I took Fred

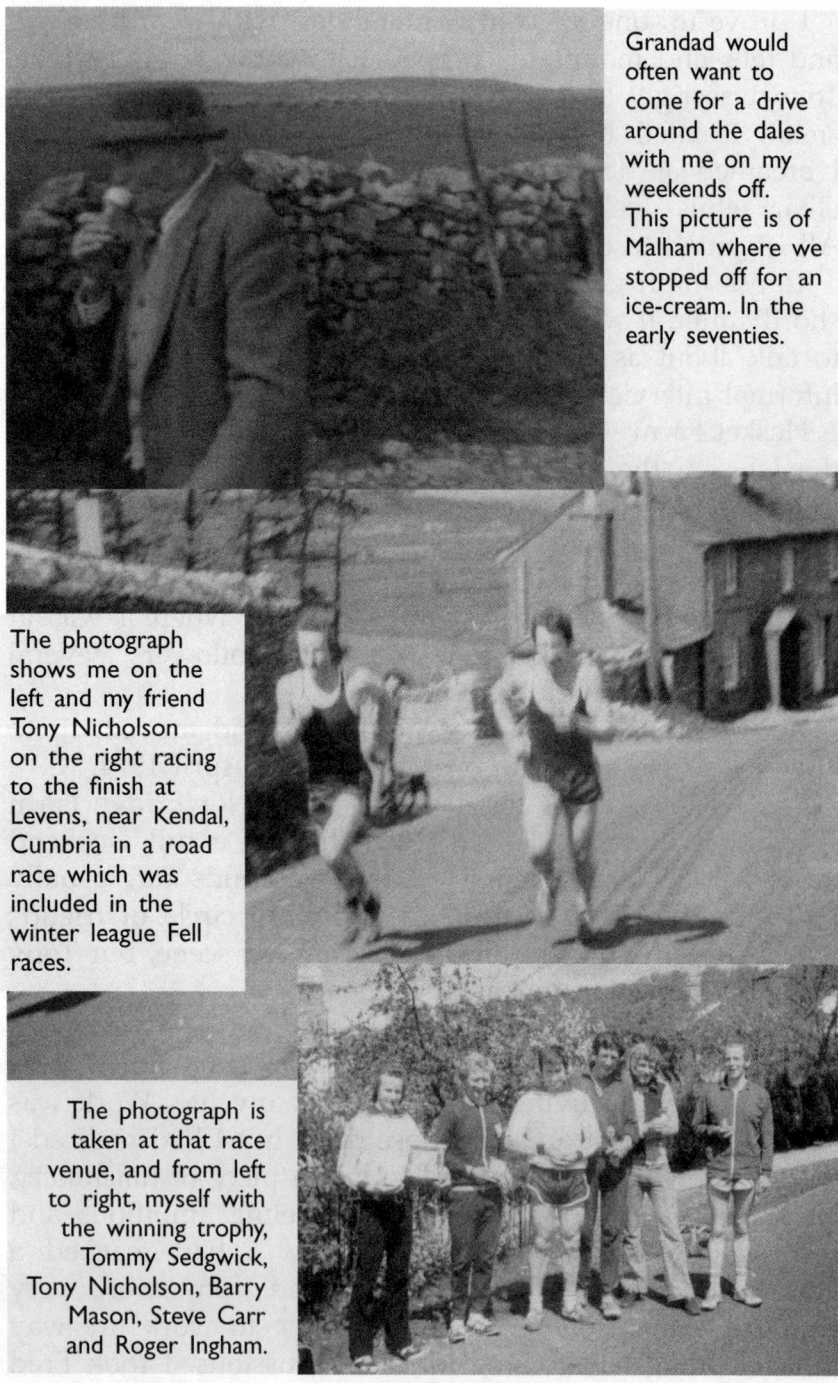

Grandad would often want to come for a drive around the dales with me on my weekends off. This picture is of Malham where we stopped off for an ice-cream. In the early seventies.

The photograph shows me on the left and my friend Tony Nicholson on the right racing to the finish at Levens, near Kendal, Cumbria in a road race which was included in the winter league Fell races.

The photograph is taken at that race venue, and from left to right, myself with the winning trophy, Tommy Sedgwick, Tony Nicholson, Barry Mason, Steve Carr and Roger Ingham.

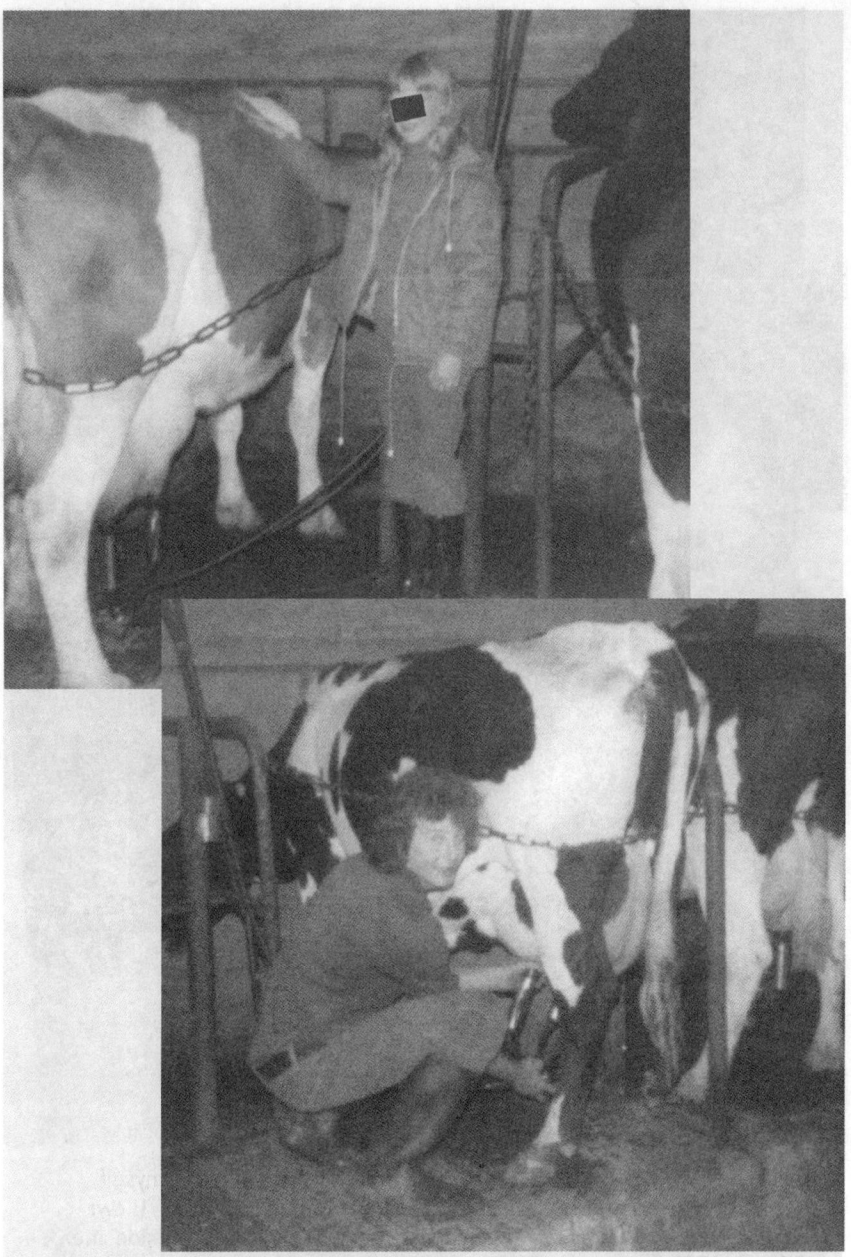

Me milking in parlour adapters at Hesket Farm, Dacre, Penrith, with Paula above who had come up to spend the holiday with me. 1974-1975.

An event Tony introduced me to was coal carrying. This is myself receiving "The Tony Nicholson Perpetual Trophy" The World 1 cwt Bag Carrying Race for the third consecutive year. Tony is beside me. 1976 to 1978.

Me with the first prize shield I had won at the winter league Fell races in the lakes, sat on my first new car I had bought whilst working at Hesket farm (Ford Escort) £900. 1974-1975.

Me with Darren at Burnsal as I took him a drive round the dales in my new Ford Escort 1974-1976.

Me clearing the first wall up the hillside in the Kilnsey Show Fell Race.

Stephen Lockwood

These photographs were taken at Hollywell Green, Halifax. Of myself in the centre of a three man team competing in a coal race around my home village of Stainland on June 2nd 1974. The Gentleman in the suit to the left was our local MP Austin Mitchell who set the race off at Hollywell Green, 11AM. I had arrived in my work clothes after driving down from Hesket farm, Dacre, Penrith, after milking 100 cows that morning, not having time to change. I completed the two mile course winning the event for our local pub landlady.

THE WESTMORLAND GAZETTE, APRIL 4, 1975

ATHLETICS

Reeves back with easy victory

Last season's top professional runner, Fred Reeves of Coniston, returned to the sport on Sunday to win the Helme Fell Race at Oxenholme.

He finished more than a minute ahead of Steve Lockwood of Penrith over the five-mile course, with Tommy Sedgwick, New Hutton, back in third place.

The handicap event was won by Lockwood with R. Clive, Kendal, second; G. Moffat, Sedbergh, third, and N. Woof, Sedbergh, fourth.

The boys' under-14 race was won by R. Swidenbank, of Kendal, with P. Mangan, Kendal, second; B. Armstrong, Kendal, third and G. Scott, Ulverston, fourth.

THE WESTMORLAND GAZETTE, MAY 16, 1975

Lockwood wins points league

Steve Lockwood of Penrith, won the Kendal Sports Committee's final league race on Sunday to make sure of topping this year's points table.

Over a course of five and a half miles, he won from Tony Nicholson, of Penrith, in a time of 24 minutes 30 seconds with Tom Sedgwick, New Hutton, third.

Final points table—1 S.Lockwood; 2 T. Nicholson; 3 T. Sedgwick; 4 B. Mason, Nether Kellett; 5 S. Carr, Kendal; 6 R. Ingham, Skipton.

Graham Moffat, Sedbergh, clinched the Under 17 table with N. Woof, Sedbergh, second and P. Cueto, Maryport, third, ahead of J. Stott, Ambleside and C. Taylforth, Hawkshead.

The first six in the Under 14 table are: 1—B. Armstrong, Ambleside; 2 J. Syms, Gargrave; 3 R. Swindenbank, Burneside; 4 M. Armstrong, Milnthorpe; 5 P. Mangan, Kendal; 6 C. Nicholson, Kendal.

12—THE HERALD, SATURDAY, MARCH 15, 1975

TROUTBECK MAN'S CROSS-COUNTRY VICTORY

Troutbeck (Penrith) runner Tony Nicholson was among winners of cross-country races held by Kendal Sports Committee at the weekend.

In the men's event Steve Lockwood led the way over the first lap, but his much improved stable-mate, Nicholson, stepped up his pace to take the lead and finished 170 yards ahead.

RESULTS

Men — 1 Tony Nicholson, Penrith; 2 Steve Lockwood, Penrith; 3 Barry Mason, Nether Kellet, Carnforth. Time: 17min. 23sec. for 3 miles (new record time).

Boys under 17 — 1 Pete Cueto, Maryport; 2 Graham Moffat, Sedbergh; 3 Nick Woof, Sedbergh.

Boys under 14 — 1 Bruce Armstrong, Ambleside; 2 Jerry Syms, Gargrave; 3 Chris. Nicholson, Kendal.

The points table at the halfway stage is as follows:

MEN

	Points
Steve Lockwood, Penrith	28
Tom Sedgewick, New Hutton, Kendal	23
Tony Nicholson, Penrith	19
Barry Mason, Nether Kellet	10
Steve Carr, Kendal	9
Rodger Ingham, Skipton	8

FASTEST WAITER IN LAKELAND SERVED UP AN ACE AT RUSLAND

THE LAKE DISTRICT'S fastest waiter, Steve Lockwood, served up his best fell-running performance at Rusland on Saturday to win his first big trophy.

Against strong competition from Chris Hartley of Seathwaite and Harvey Gott of Kendal, Steve powered his way through wet grass and up and down a Rusland fellside to win the Reg Harrison Trophy in the men's fell race.

Earlier rain had lashed down on the Whitestock Meadow site of the 93rd annual Rusland Valley Horticultural Society show and sports and provided soft going for both hound trails and the flat and fell races.

Steve, who trains daily with a three-mile run to his work as a waiter at the Tarn Howes Hotel, Hawkshead, virtually sprinted away at the start of the fell race. He said afterwards: "I knew that if I did not break away right at the start Chris would overtake me.

NEVER BEFORE

"I knew I had to get in front going up and get in the lead for the down stretch because Chris is fast coming down. I have never run on this fell before."

Chris Hartley, a farmer, was second and Harvey Gott, a shoe factory worker, who had earlier won the men's one-mile race in four min. 22 sec., arrived third.

Saturday's event introduced for the first time the under-14 boys' fell race which was won by Andrew Brockbank of Millom.

Philip Robinson, 14, of Elm Tree Farm, Preston Patrick, won the under-17-year boys' fell race to take home the Lawson Challenge Trophy. "It was quite an easy race. The cool weather helped a lot," he said.

Rusland Show chairman Mr Gordon Wilkinson said the annual event is going from strength to strength.

Despite a wet start, with competitors and officials being forced to run for shelter on several occasions, the event became sunnier as the afternoon progressed, with a children's fancy dress parade, boys' wrestling, tug-o-war contests and other attractions.

A RECORD

In the horticultural section entries totalled more than 600 and proved to be a record for the show.

A first prize marrow, bigger than a rugby football was exhibited by B. S. Smith of Rockside, Bouth.

An entry of two peaches produced by J. Johnson of Rusland was declared the most outstanding exhibit and won the Amateur Gardening Red Ribbon.

Mr Wilf Procter's three-year old hound Bandrake Lena won him the John Ormandy Challenge Trophy by a two-dog-length lead over Reveille in the old dogs trail.

Loyal owned by John Hutchinson of Backbarrow won the puppies trail by a distance, to win the Joe Wilkinson Perpetual Challenge Cup.

TROPHIES

Lawson Challenge Trophy (boys' fell race under 17 years) Philip Robinson of Preston Patrick; Reg Harrison Trophy (men's fell race)—Steve Lockwood of Hawkshead; John Ormandy Memorial Challenge Trophy—Wilf Procter of Oxen Park with hound Bandrake Lena; Joe Wilkinson Perpetual Challenge Cup (puppies trail)—John Hutchinson of Backbarrow with Loyal.

Amateur Gardening Red Ribbon Award (most outstanding horticultural exhibit)—J. Johnson of The Archways, Rusland; Martin Stokes Challenge Cup: J. Johnson; Young Farmers Club Trophy for Girls—Ruth Johnson, The Archways, Rusland; Young Farmers Club trophy for Boys—David Fletcher of Laburnum Cottage, Satterthwaite.

Against strong competition from Chris Hartley of Seathwaite and Harvey Gott of Kendal, Steve powered his way through wet grass and up and down a Rusland fellside to win the Reg Harrison Trophy in the men's fell race.

up on his offer to let me train with him, should I decide to move.

Fred lived at Coniston, which was much more challenging fell running country, but there were few dairy farms in this area, and so I had to make a career change. Meeting all the fell runners over the last few years had introduced me to social evenings along the way, such as dinner dances, and although still quite reserved in new company, I was losing my shyness, making it easier to explore new avenues. Coniston was a thriving tourist place, and had a good hotel trade. So, after a heart-wrenching decision with John, as we sat on a bale of straw, I decided to leave Hesket Farm and farming for good.

By now, I had arranged my 21st birthday party, with the help of Tony, so John and Margaret were invited, along with friends I had made over the past four years. It was held on Sunday, 4th May 1975 at a country inn between Keswick and Grasmere, which Tony had frequented during his running career. Although every effort had been made by friends for the occasion, which I thoroughly enjoyed, I can still vividly remember a sense of sadness during that eve, as not one member of my family had accepted my invitation.

On Monday, 28th April 1975, I began my first job as a hotel porter in Ambleside. After just a few weeks, I realised how much catering had to offer and moved to a higher class establishment at Tarn Hows, just outside Coniston, working as a commis waiter. By this time, I was aware how quickly I was able to move from one job to another. However much I liked working somewhere, there was always a new challenge, and unfortunately this became a kind of roller-coaster which I was to experience for many more years.

The summer of 1975 was extremely hot. I recall meeting Fred near Donald Campbell's monument in Coniston very early one morning, so that we could run in the cool dew before the heat of the day. Our route took us through beautiful woodland and over fells before reaching Tarn

Hows, where I would leave Fred so I could begin my day's work at Tarn Hows Hotel, serving breakfasts. Fred would continue and inform me at our next meet of his overall mileage. I would increase my training by running home after late dinner shifts, which could be in the black of night, any time between 11.00 p.m. and 1.00 a.m., yet still very warm after the heat of the day, and some nights enjoying the moonlight.

This was to be the fittest time of my life, peaking in my running and thoroughly enjoying it, along with my work. There was also another interest taking place. I was beginning my first serious courtship, with the cook at the hotel where I worked. It had never bothered me being a virgin up to this point in life, but when something comes naturally, like my running, I just had to follow it. This was to turn into quite an intense relationship over the next few years.

Susan was an attractive girl, the eldest of five, and a farmer's daughter from Hawkshead, just down the road from the hotel. We would often return to her parents' farm, where we all chatted as we ate home-cooked food, served up by her mother in a cosy old farmhouse kitchen.

Though I was enjoying the experience catering was offering me, I could feel the tug of the outdoors drawing me as I would steal a few moments at the hotel dining room window on a hot summer's day, watching any farming activity that caught my eye.

The hotel was luxurious. The thick wool pile carpeted dining room would draw my feet until they ached, as I waited on customers through long late shifts. At the end of service, removing my bow tie, jacket and shoes was heaven, as I changed into my running gear to flee over the fells, feet barely touching the ground as I pranced mile after mile, pretending I was part of the fauna that inhabited them.

During busy periods on the farm I would be asked to lend a hand, and would find it difficult to resist if there was some free time. Damson picking, hay timing or anything that kept me in touch with my roots – it was life feeding off me in my prime, and me feeding off life.

October saw the hotel season coming to an end. Staff had the option to stay on through the winter and decorate, but I chose to come back to Yorkshire, and took a herdsman's job for the winter, giving me time to find out if I would want to return to catering. Susan and I kept in touch, visiting and writing. This was to continue for almost four years, as I returned to catering, travelling between the Lake District and Yorkshire; working in different hotels.

Since moving up to Hesket Farm in 1974, I had been carrying with me, in my suitcase as well as my mind, something that was weighing very heavily and that I desperately wanted to shed. I was so very happy in everything I saw, touched and the air I breathed, but I just could not let anyone get too close for fear they would find my inner sadness. I did not want to share sadness, only happiness, which I had found in the Lake District and Yorkshire Dales, through friends and places, but conversations would lead me to reveal a little, before embarrassingly clamming up or changing the subject.

Whilst living and working at my herdsman's job at Raybridge Farm, I made every effort to get home and spend time with mum and the family on days off. She found it difficult raising the rest of the family by herself, and I was sensitive to her needs. Since they were unable to afford a holiday or even a few days away, I would often take her and my brothers or sisters for a day out up in the Dales or Lakes, sometimes driving around the areas where I worked or was fell running. She was always interested in whatever I was doing or wherever I was living. My wages were low and mum would often contribute towards petrol or food. A very nervous person in company, she was happy for me just to drive around and show her places. She was just so pleased to have my company and would delight in telling anyone back home of her day out.

Things would be fine if I paid regular visits home, but that was not always possible, and any length of time without a visit would result in a letter from mum. Depending on what had been happening at home, the contents would vary from informing me of any recent events, to making me feel very guilty at being away. There were times when I found car repairs difficult and mum would send cash in a letter towards the bill. We always seemed to know when either of us was in need of help, but somehow mum had developed a knack of making me feel extremely guilty about her, which left things bitter-sweet.

My move to Hesket Farm in 1974 was hard for her, and although I still continued my regular visits, I was now two hours away and mum found that distance difficult. I was to begin receiving letters that upset me deeply; references being made as to how she had raised us all by herself and suddenly, as though I had never had any thought for her, telling me there was no thanks for it. I had been here before – those letters that arrived in Somerset when I was fifteen years old were now back to haunt me. The contents eventually became more poisonous. Sometimes I would leave them for days before opening them, and with a glimmer of hope would risk it, only to find words, some quite strong, that would reduce me to tears as the emotional knife went in. However much mum tried to hurt me now though, my saving grace was that I did not feel homesick as before. I had moved on in life, and did not feel cut off, as I now had a car to visit home.

I was now twenty-two, and in a relationship. It occurred to me that I was going to have to be very strong in order to make someone happy, whilst trying to keep peace with mum. Neither Susan nor anyone else ever knew the contents of the letters I received and kept, some of which I returned. I introduced her to mum and she was very understanding, but mum found the situation difficult, eventually showing her resentment.

During 1978, I had met many people through catering; I became very friendly with two of them. The Lake District is popular with Geordies, and easy to reach by car. The fact we were almost resorting to sign language because I had never encountered this species before did not matter, because their easy, open hospitality more than compensated. I was referred to as "Yorky", and Jan and Ian became my very dear friends.

As another season drew to a close, I was aware of the familiar pattern of moving on for the winter, which usually meant back to Yorkshire. Jan and Ian enquired what my intentions were, and invited me to stay the winter with them at North Shields. I gratefully accepted and, with their hospitality, went on to enjoy to the full some of the most exciting times of my twenties, often looking back with very fond memories. Sadly, Ian is no longer with us, but Jan and I have remained very good friends.

Chapter Eight

Two years before meeting Jan and Ian, I had been working close to home in Yorkshire, between February 1976 and October 1977, under the supervision of a very talented maître d'hôtel whom I had known previously, and from whom I could gain much experience.

The summer of 1976 was a repeat of 1975, with very long, hot days, running into a heat wave over most of the summer. I missed being in the Lakes for the summer, but it turned out that things had to be. Susan and I continued seeing each other, and I was able to spend some time with mum, as well as visiting my grandparents.

Over the years I had been away from home, I was aware that the rest of my brothers and sisters were feeling the demands of mum. She had moved house several times and there was often a man on the scene. So my being around again eased things a little.

My grandparents were in their early eighties, and had begun to find life hard at their farmhouse cottage in the country, where they had spent some happy years. Mum and my two aunties had to decide what was to be done, and in the end mum managed to persuade my grandparents to move into a ground floor flat closer to the town centre. It was easier for them in some ways, but somehow they did not seem to settle, and shortly after, on the 24th April 1976, aged 80, my Nan passed away after suffering a heavy stroke. This left my grandad devastated and pining desperately after Nan.

There was quite a bit of upset between mum and my two

aunties. Mum's middle sister decided grandad would stay in a cottage next door to her so she could care for him; this seemed to make sense, but did not bode well with mum, who felt pushed aside and restricted by the decisions of her two sisters.

My Nan's death brought my first experience of a funeral. As always, these are very sad times for all families but it also proved to be an extremely difficult time throughout the service, as mum was unable to cope, and practically went into convulsions through getting so upset. Following her loss, in the days, weeks and months after, we all rallied to give her the support she needed, but mum just went deeper into depression.

During this time, grandad was failing. I recall visiting, and seeing him in bed, so pathetically weak, rambling and helpless. It cut me to the core to see the only man in my life for whom I had total respect in such a state, the man who was so solid and always there for me through my childhood; who had shared bars of chocolate with me; tickled me to make me laugh; told me he would take his belt off to me if he thought I was pushing my luck; let me wear his nightshirt to settle down to sleep in their cosy cottage, when times were difficult in my home; and then, as I grew, sharing rides in my car up the Yorkshire Dales, stopping for an ice cream, and telling me tales of his farming days; and seeing his contentment at being able to get out for the day and then to be taken back to Nan.

I left him in the care of my auntie, and as I walked outside, tried to be grown-up, thinking how strong I was going to have to be; whilst at the same time hoping grandad would not have to suffer, knowing what a proud man he was.

Just twelve months and three days after losing Nan, on 27th April 1977, grandad passed away peacefully. I cannot explain how I dealt with the situation between that day and the funeral; except finding it difficult to accept the loss. I was numb, and everything suddenly didn't seem real. Not having the strength I had at Nan's funeral, I broke down uncontrollably as the coffin went out of sight. Standing outside, I felt no shame for my tears, but just very alone as my world had fallen apart. The family eventually gathered me in as we left and returned to my auntie's for sandwiches.

Since leaving home I had always kept a diary of my places of work, and of my mileage while fell running. I had kept up my running through these difficult times. It was my way of coping, out there in the open spaces and with the smells of Mother Nature. Time was slowly healing things at home now.

The restaurant where I had been working with the maître d'hôtel was sold, and after trying a few more places locally, I decided to move on. Catering is a restless trade, which had seemed to become a way of life for me.

My first thoughts were to return to the Lake District, but I also knew there were good opportunities abroad and so, whilst applying for various positions, I took a low-key job on a static caravan site between Penrith and Keswick, only one mile away from where my friend Tony lived. Three letters arrived shortly after, confirming I had been accepted for the positions I had applied for. Two were in the Channel Islands and one at Lake Lucerne in Switzerland. A combination of excitement and nerves came over me. The maître d'hôtel had polished me, and I knew I was capable of the high standards the Swiss required. It was decision time, but after informing mum, guilt got the better of me, and I shall never know what could have been. I completed the season at the caravan site, where I met Jan and Ian before joining them in North Shields in early October 1978.

Jan and Ian could not have made me more welcome. Both they and Jan's parents, of whom I also became very fond, treat me as part of the family. In general, I found the local people very hospitable, and Ian was very good at involving me in many of the local activities.

I began work as a chef de rang at a busy businessmen's hotel between Newcastle and Morpeth. Jan and Ian were

Ian on the left and Jan on the right with their dog Moss, myself in the centre. Taken on St Mary's Island on the east coast just above North Shields 1978.

very flattering about my culinary skills, and so I would repay their compliments by making meals for them, as they came home from work before I began my evening shift. Jan worked for a local insurance company, and Ian worked on the local fishing docks.

Just as my grandad taught me how to savour every morsel of food when eating a meal, I have always believed life's pleasant experiences should be savoured too, and in my case, none less than indulging in langoustines during the time I spent with Jan and Ian. Ian was responsible for the catches of fish coming in on the trawlers, and would have to be on the docks at unearthly hours to check them in. He always let me know when langoustines were due in, and I would be at the ready, down there with him, often very late at night. It was an insight into a way of life I had only seen on the news on TV, but something totally different to mine. As I stood there on the dockside watching Ian supervising as the huge nets of langoustines were hoisted from the boats, I savoured the moments I was able to experience as the hustle and bustle of the fishermen's excitement grew if it was a large catch. This would be dealt with immediately, as more staff would be clocking on to prepare this and other kinds of fish for the early morning hours of trading.

What may have seemed routine to Ian at the time seemed fascinating to me. He probably little knew what gratitude I felt for his giving me this opportunity, which may seem to many to be no great thing, but to a lad from Yorkshire, who had led a very sheltered life and was just spreading his wings, boy, that's what friends like Ian are for.

The icing on the cake was when Ian would give me a whole box of langoustines to take home and prepare for our meals. This happened on regular occasions during my stay with them, and memories of meal times with them over langoustines and sherry trifle will stay with me forever.

Before moving over to Jan and Ian's, Susan had made it known to me that she was wanting to become serious, by way of settling down to marriage. I knew I was not ready for that, and after a few discussions, shortly after going to Jan and Ian's, I received a 'phone call from Susan, during which we both agreed to terminate our relationship. It was very difficult and, looking back, I don't think I knew how much I had really hurt Susan at the time. It was my first relationship, and it did feel painful knowing that I was the one who ended it. But something so strong was telling me to move on in life.

It was now late December 1978. I had been with Jan and Ian almost three months. The hotel was busy with Christmas fare and I was just about understanding some broad Geordie dialect among the staff. Then, one evening, during food service, I was summoned to the telephone. I cannot remember who made the call, whether it was mum or some other member of the family, but the brief I was given put me in total shock. One of my brothers (Keith, aged 22) had been found dead. I left work and made my way to Jan and Ian's house. They would not let me drive alone back down to mum in Yorkshire, and with great concern, both came down with me.

Mum was at that time living in a flat, which was part of an old converted nursing home on the outskirts of Halifax. As we entered the room, I recall mum sitting in one corner, unable to stand, still in shock, and only half the frame of person she was. The weight seemed literally to have come off overnight after hearing the news. Jan sat beside her and comforted her. This was now mum's third loss of close family in three years. It is only now as I write, that I realise how strong she would have had to be at that time.

Sunday, 9th November 2003. After only a couple of attempts this year, I have been unable to write more than a few pages due to a heavy work load in my employment. I have now completed the third phase of a large project, which has left me greatly satisfied and feeling I can return to my writing, hopefully with more consistency, in the evenings and weekends through the winter months.

After Jan and Ian left for home, it still had not registered with any of us quite what had happened. I remember an awful feeling of helplessness and loneliness we must have all been feeling at the time. With mum living alone, and no man to support her, we all had to draw on our own strengths and help her through this.

Throughout our lives, I recall mum always taking on a darkened attitude in the weeks leading up to Christmas, saying tragedies always occur at Christmas time. But I always loved Christmas and was determined to enjoy it in my own way as a child. Now this crisis made it even more difficult.

It was the week before Christmas, and the main concern was that funeral arrangements had to be made as quickly as possible so Keith was not left over the Christmas period. Keith had been found on Saturday, 23rd December 1978, washed up on the coast at Bridlington. It has never been known how he met his death, whether it was suicide or other circumstances we will never know, but what added to all our distress, and particularly mum's, was that it was announced on the television news. The service and cremation went ahead at the same place as nanna's and grandad's over the last two years.

After the funeral, my eldest brother had to return home to Somerset, and I had to travel back to Newcastle to my work. This left Paula, now 17 years old, who was living locally in lodgings; Darren, 21 years old, also living and working locally; and our youngest sister, Sandra, who was just eight years old, living with mum. Although left totally distraught, mum had Sandra to care for, which gave her something to focus on and helped her through the days, weeks and years ahead.

A short time after the funeral, I was finding it very difficult to come to terms with what had happened. I prayed so hard, hoping for answers. Why? Why? Why? I kept praying, unbeknown to the rest of the family. Sometimes I felt so exhausted but never lost faith. Then, one time as I was praying, I walked to my bedside and picked up my bible, which I had always kept with me from junior school. Although I had never read it or understood it, I always felt it a comfort to me just being there. I will never forget the force that came over me to open it. It opened at one page. I recall having no feeling of wanting to search through it, but was instantly focused on two words *"I cried"*. So I read on, and from that day, have felt my prayers were answered. I read it over and over, whilst a coldness ran over me knowing Keith had found life so very difficult. It was Psalm 142 – I called it Keith's Psalm – and it read:

"I cried unto the Lord with my voice;
With my voice unto the Lord did I make my supplication.
I poured out my complaint before him;
I shewed before him my trouble.
When my spirit was overwhelmed within me, then thou
*   knewest my path.*

In the way wherein I walked have they privily laid a snare
*   for me.*
I looked on my right hand, and beheld, but there was no
*   man that would know me:*
Refuge failed me; no man cared for my soul.
I cried unto thee, O Lord:
I said, Thou art my refuge
And my portion in the land of the living.
Attend unto my cry; for I am brought very low:
Deliver me from my persecutors; for they are stronger than
*   I.*
Bring my soul out of prison, that I may praise thy name:
The righteous shall compass me about;
For thou shalt deal bountifully with me."
(Authorized Version of The Bible)

Chapter Nine

I found it difficult thinking of mum and how she was struggling by herself with Sandra, whilst still very tender from bereavement. So my plans of promotion within the hotel where I was working came to a sudden end, as I made arrangements to leave on the 18th February 1979 and come home to mum for a holiday. I had had a wonderful time with Jan and Ian and it was very difficult having to leave them. They very kindly arranged to visit mum again in two weeks' time, and so spent the weekend of 2nd to 4th March 1979 with us. I was still single, with no commitments, and mum looked on me as a father figure for Sandra, feeling more settled when I was around.

The week before I arrived at mum's she had been making great efforts to rescue a Staffordshire bull terrier, which was wasting away through neglect by its owner and a serious illness. Mum had managed to make special arrangements with the landlord of her flat and was allowed to keep her. She had to raise £60.00 for a life-saving operation, which was a success, and "Sooty", as she was called, settled in, with mum treating her like a baby. We were all very fond of Sooty, who I'm sure filled a very empty space in mum's life at the time. She went on to give mum and all of us a great deal of pleasure before fading away from old age.

Throughout the sad times over the last three years I had still managed to continue my training for the fell races and was averaging forty miles a week. I was twenty-five years old and feeling at my peak. My friend Tony was also getting me involved in a pet sport of his known as "coal

Lucky Sooty settles in

FOUR-YEAR-OLD Sooty is lucky to be alive.

Neglected by her owner and wasting through a serious illness she was rescued by Mrs Laura Finlay, of 9, Stansfield Grange, Triangle.

Mrs Finlay called in the RSPCA and paid more than £60 — the proceeds from the sale of a car — for a life-saving operation. She made special arrangements with the landlords of her rented flat so that the Staffordshire bull terrier bitch could stay with her, but said she was prepared to move if necessary to keep her.

During the worst of the crisis, Sooty weighed little more than half her normal weight, had a high temperature and was unable to walk. Now she is fit and healthy, though still nervous of strangers.

Mrs Finlay, who got to know her about a year ago, said: "I took an interest in her, and to me she was a baby. I won't part with her."

Mrs Finlay is pictured with Sooty.

This is Mum with her dog Sooty who she rescued in 1979. Lucky Sooty!

carrying", which he excelled at. I was hungry for my own space. Space away from the sad times that always seemed to hang over my home life. Running on the open fells of The Lakes and The Dales gave me that space in abundance, with exhilaration running through me from the hairs on my head to every bone in my body, it was my "elixir". I was fit now and very aware of it; taking every opportunity to run wherever I stayed and whomsoever I stayed with; my shorts, vest and trainers always went with me.

My concern now was finding work. Mum would take on a low ebb as always when it came to me leaving after a visit, which made it difficult. Although there will always be some special childhood memories for me of Halifax, after the loss of my grandparents I quickly outgrew it, and always knew I would one day come to live in North Yorkshire. I made the decision to take a waiter's job in a restaurant called "Long Ashes" near Grassington on 8th March 1979. Beautiful fell running country, and easy distance for me to get to visit mum.

There were two things dominating my life: mum, and fell running. Work was always fitted around these two, and at the cost of carving out a secure career for myself. Whenever I began to make progress at work, something would happen at home that mum found difficult to cope with. There would be letters or 'phone calls that would weigh me down with feelings of guilt. So I would turn to my great escape – running. Wherever I worked or whomever I stayed with, my running was always well received as a topic of conversation, which helped me to keep the happenings at home firmly in the background.

Looking back, I can see I was literally running away from what I found so difficult to cope with at home. All I craved was to meet happy people, engage in interesting conversation, and make light of the world around me. Catering gave me all this. Yes, every family has its difficult times, but most seemed to be in balance with good ones. Throughout my childhood there had been lots of difficulties.

This was my playtime, albeit a little late, and I was making the most of it.

My accommodation was included with the job at the restaurant, which was a basic static caravan sited behind the building at the foot of the limestone fells. It had Calor Gas, but I prided myself on being hardy and rarely used it. Winter still had a firm grip with heavy snowfalls that month; it was picturesque, and stunning training sessions followed in both the winter and summer of 1979.

Since leaving school I had been on a roller-coaster; in and out of jobs at a rate that left family and friends mesmerised, whilst it also became a great source of amusement to all, including my best friend Tony, who still reminds me of such times as we share laughs. However, deep down I was now becoming concerned as to how I could secure myself in employment. I was now twenty-five years old and had had more than that number of years in jobs – twenty-eight in total to date. "Long Ashes" was run by a friendly family, who were all going their own ways in work and so once again I had to move on. In December of that year I left and yes, returned to mum, temporarily.

I had become very health conscious, particularly with my diet. This was at a time when wholefood diets and shops were seen as somewhat cranky. I would travel miles to seek out good wholemeal food and health shops. Other jobs followed and, looking back, I am amazed that at no time was I ever unemployed. The pace of changeover would be so quick, that I would sometimes never unpack my suitcases. Knowing that this was an area of my life that I had lost control over bothered me.

Somehow, I had managed to save over £1,000.00 throughout 1979, and decided I was going to have a holiday. We all knew mum was going to find this Christmas very difficult, so I stayed with her over the period but, on Sunday, 27th January 1980, I flew from Manchester Airport to Austria on a seven-day skiing holiday. On my return, I felt as though I had really stretched those wings, and found

Me, third from right on a skiing holiday in Soll, Austria 1st Feb 1980.
It was a magical holiday just at the time I needed one.

myself longing to settle down. It was over twelve months since I had broken up with Susan, and I felt I was ready for another relationship.

By September 1980 I found myself in the position of restaurant manager at a 3-star country hotel in the Yorkshire Dales: "The Falcon Manor" at Settle. The position fitted me like a glove. I had gained a lot of confidence in myself since those days back on the farm, and I relished the responsibilities that went with this job. My employers were an ex-farming family, so we had lots in common, including an appreciation of good food.

However, my life was to gain an even faster pace. Functions, weddings, à la carte restaurant; all this kept me working into the small hours, and my boss, being a typical farmer, wanted his pound of flesh. Weekend breaks in October were being offered at a special rate, and on one such evening, as I was taking the restaurant, three people walked in, whom I seated in the bay window. They were mother, father and daughter Helen. As we discussed the menu it was a quiet evening, and so I decided to serve them myself. Something special happened, and in September the following year, Helen and I were married.

Helen and her parents had been on a weekend break from London, where they all three lived together. On their return, Helen and I immediately made arrangements to keep in contact by post, telephone and visits. After an evening meal in a restaurant on Monday, 29th December 1980, I asked Helen to marry me. Helen accepted, and we became engaged the following year.

Helen and I both enjoyed walking. The scenery was beautiful, with lots of crisp days and coverings of snow. Thursday, 26th February 1981 was such a day. We packed our rucksacks with sandwiches and walked over the Yorkshire Dales to Malham, discussing our wedding plans. The date was set: Saturday, 26th September 1981.

Helen had trained in pharmacy work, and so I managed to find her a job in the chemist's in the village where I worked. My accommodation was a room in the hotel, so we both agreed to rent a house and set up home in the village. Helen would stay up into the small hours, waiting for me to finish my shift, which I found very unfair on her. It was not an ideal job for me to be in when just starting married life. We were deeply in love and wanted to spend as much time together as possible.

One of the Freemasons I served at the hotel had a dairy farm in the next village and offered me a job. It was a step back for me at the time, but it meant we could be together more and so, on Sunday, 21st June 1981 I finished work at "The Falcon Manor" and began my herdsman's job the following day.

The 26th September arrived, and yes, I can still honestly say, without any doubt, at that time it was the happiest day of my life. Helen was simply beautiful. We were married in the village church with a reception at a restaurant a few miles away, followed by a honeymoon in Wales and then in

Page 2—CRAVEN NEWS, March 5, 1981

MAY WE RECOMMEND . . *OUR EATING OUT GUIDE*

FALCON SETTLES ON FINE FOOD

The popularity of the Falcon Manor at Settle is soaring — and with good reason.

Owners — Chris and Doris Riley — have grabbed the cost of living by the throat and have somehow managed to provide a superb four-course dinner menu, followed by coffee and mints, at the seemingly impossible all-inclusive price of just £5.70 per person.

A party of four from the Craven News dined at the Falcon on Sunday evening and all decided to substitute the set main course for a variety of steaks including the delicious steak au poivre. An unexpected touch was that one of the vegetables was aubergines in cheese sauce, not usually to be found as a set veg.

The beauty of the Falcon is that although there is a choice on the set menu, alternatives can be chosen from the a la carte menu — admittedly at extra cost — to give a really wide and impressive selection.

HOT DISH

One of my colleagues started with a seafood platter au gratin, a hot dish which she found excellent and highly recommends.

Although there is a choice of more than 70 wines, including vintage champagne, we plumped for one of the house wines, a Valpolicelli, which complemented the steaks to a tee.

By the time the sweet course came round, only two of the party felt able to tackle it and decided to have two small portions

of cheesecake. All in all, a first class meal excellently prepared and served in a personable manner and working out at a highly reasonable cost of less than £9 per person — top food at top value.

Mr and Mrs Riley have five daughters — four of whom work at the Falcon full or part-time and the finely-appointed restaurant exudes a friendly and personal atmosphere.

Open seven days a week with evening serving from 7.30 to 9.30, the Falcon has been awarded two star rating in both the R.A.C. and A.A. 1981 guides. So fly out to the Falcon.

Picture shows Ian Horsman, chef; Stephen Lockwood, head waiter; Mr and Mrs Riley, and three of their daughters, Kathryn, Carol and Gillian.

The Falcon Manor Hotel, Settle, North Yorkshire where I both established myself as head waiter and met Helen in 1981.

London with Helen's parents. After ten days we returned to Settle to live.

I must say at this stage there had been, to say the least, fragile moments with mum leading up to the wedding. Helen handled this carefully without any malice whatsoever, but with a degree of bewilderment that mum could be putting so much pressure on us at this time. On the day, I barely glanced as I passed mum's vacant seat on the top table at our wedding reception, as she firmly refused to come to the wedding.

During the next eighteen months I started up my own outside catering business. We were desperate to start buying our own house, but found that the business was not making enough money to get us on the first rung of the housing ladder, as the already expensive properties in Settle continued to go through the roof and way beyond what we could ever afford.

The catering unit we brought custom made from Scarborough. Helen is in the unit. I am on the left with my partner on the right, as we were ready to leave Scarborough.

We had made some very good friends in Settle, and in particular our next-door neighbours, Sheila and Gordon. We both loved living in Settle but knew we had now to say our goodbyes. Helen did not want to move too far away, but the decision making was left to me. My hope was that we would renovate a property somewhere, make a profit, and move back to Settle. Because I knew the prices of property were much cheaper near Halifax and I knew the area, I suggested I went down for a couple of weeks to look for property and work for us both. I recall Helen being very distraught at the idea of us being apart whilst I searched, and I look back at this decision in my life with some sadness. What I had seemed to overlook was that I was not just uprooting myself to move on in life now, but also my wife. It was from now on that I came to realise, as most people will, how difficult it becomes to make decisions as you go through life.

Sandra on the swings across the road whilst on one of her stays with us.

A couple of weeks later we were attending an interview on the outskirts of Halifax. After two interviews, we were the successful applicants for the steward and stewardess positions at "Mount Skip" golf club. In March 1983 Helen's parents hired a Luton van in London, and drove up to help us move the few pieces of secondhand furniture we had, as we left Settle behind.

The location of the golf club was panoramic. It was set just above the tree line, against the moorland heather, some 900 feet above sea level, high on the Pennines above Hebden Bridge, and extremely exposed. The approach road edged the very top of the valley below, taking in views for miles around. On getting out of our vehicles, Helen's parents' faces showed a mixture of being aghast, excited and bewildered. There followed some friction in conversation over their concern for Helen's future. We were all aware

Mount Skip Golf Club with its four large windows overlooking the valley – the recessed centre of the building was our living accommodation. We still had our Four Wheel drive. Helen's parents Renault is parked in the foreground. 1983.

there was a lot of hard work ahead, and what's more, I was responsible, so I had to prove the venture would work.

We made the old golf house as comfortable as possible for the time we spent in it. The attraction for me was that the catering side had been run down. There was no restaurant operating or functions being held; so we wrote up menus, put our plan into action, and noses to the grindstone. The result was a golf club bursting at the seams with private functions, golfers' functions and private restaurant. Our feet never touched the ground; people were coming from all over the valley. I was completely swept along.

Between afternoon teas and bar openings we would sit in the huge plate glass bay windows of the bar lounge, which took in the expanse of moorland landscape across the valley and into Lancashire, as we watched the most spectacular sunsets for a few minutes before starting work again. The golfers were keen for us to keep the bar open all hours, so we had to be very disciplined in closing, as we still had lots of work into the small hours. By this time we were both exhausted. Helen was tremendous, both in support of me and her work, and I can only praise her efforts. However, it was not until some years later that I accidentally discovered how blind I had been in not seeing how much pressure I had put Helen under with our work load. Although I was used to the pressures of catering, not only had Helen been adjusting to living up north and wondering how I was going to earn a living, but she had now given up her chemist's work to work with me in catering.

Back in the September of 1980, as I had begun work at "The Falcon Manor", mum moved out of her flat and bought a house in the next valley to the golf club. By now she had adjusted to my marriage to Helen and they were both getting on quite well. In fact, mum became quite supportive of Helen, and became a great help to her at the golf club.

During our first two years we had great support from

the captains and councils to whom we were responsible, but towards the end of our second year, we heard through the grapevine that the next captain was very unpopular and there had been decisions made to take away some of our catering privileges. This meant that the very low combined salary we were on would not justify all the hours we were working. This came as quite a shock to me, as I was hoping we could work there for approximately five years to save enough for a deposit on a house. Consequently, we discussed looking for a house immediately, and found one further down the valley towards Halifax, on the hillside.

In November 1984 we left "Mount Skip" golf club and moved into our own house at Luddendenfoot. This was purchased with the help of a £1,000.00 gift from Helen's parents and what little money we had between us. The approach was very steep up the hillside but once there it had lovely views across the valley. It was an end terrace

The road approaching our cottage before we began work on it.

house in need of renovation, and lent itself to a cottage style.

Helen decided she did not like catering and found work at a Chemist's in Hebden Bridge. It had always been my dream to renovate a property, so I began immediately. Obviously, this did not bring in an income and I had to think of ways to earn money to allow me to work on the house. The golf club had given me an insight into working for myself, and so I was reluctant to go back into hotel work; also, we were considering starting a family.

I worked on the house full time until November 1985. A series of full and part-time jobs followed, but at least I had said goodbye to full-time catering.

Chapter Ten

Helen had made it clear to me that she did not want to move back to Settle. She had got used to being able to shop in the nearby towns, whereas we had a sixteen-mile journey from Settle to the nearest town. I now realised we could begin to put our roots down.

In 1986 Helen suffered a miscarriage, which was very upsetting for her. By now I had finished the house and started landscaping the garden. I was immediately hooked, and pursued a part-time, six-months' horticultural qualification at the local college. However, that same year, Helen became pregnant again, and on the 22nd April 1987 our son was born at the Halifax General Hospital. On the 30th August 1987, he was christened Dale John Lockwood in Luddenden Village.

I was there throughout Helen's labour and at the birth. I can only say, I could never imagine how much happiness one person could bring into someone's life; first on our wedding day, and then to give us our child. I would hope that any man in this position would not take marriage alone for granted. As for a woman: to give birth is, or at least I feel, a great show of deep love and affection towards her man. We were now a family.

Two weeks later I completed my course at college and began looking for work in horticulture. During this period I worked in a garden for a professional couple working in the field of Television. They gave me the opportunity of designing part of their garden, which became a catalyst to my newfound career.

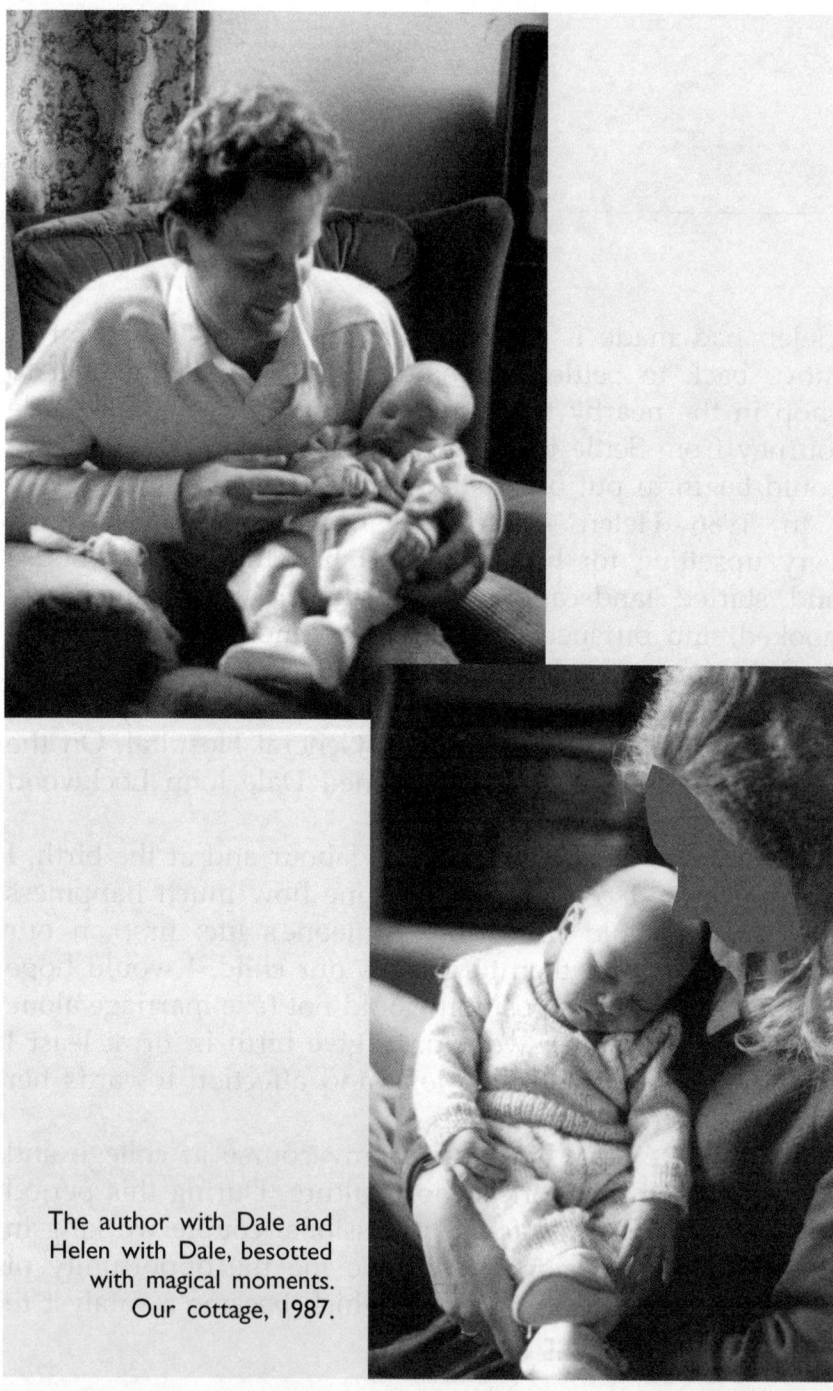

The author with Dale and
Helen with Dale, besotted
with magical moments.
Our cottage, 1987.

Whilst living at the Golf Club, we were aware of how vulnerable we were in our isolation, particularly in the late evenings when we had cashed up and were alone. We both loved the idea of a dog, and so began looking. We needed something that would guard, but I was aware that Helen was not used to dogs, and so we stayed clear of Alsatians. We looked at many breeds and in our research came across Rottweilers. There were only a few around at the time and we went to selected breeders for advice. Their nature suited our purpose. Although a fairly intimidating dog to look at, they guarded silently, with a soft nature towards their handlers.

The outcome was the most adorable, square, solid bundle of fun that we both fell for, and who came home with us at eight weeks old. Helen became very fond of him as he grew, and "Jack", as we called him, went on to win first prize in Obedience classes. He grew into a nine-stone, loveable softy, with a nature reminiscent of a Labrador. However, soon after we got Jack the breed gained in popularity, and we could not have envisaged what was to happen. The breed was used in films, portrayed as evil beasts and dangerous guard dogs; they got into the wrong hands, and consequently suffered bad press. The media had created a stigma and Rottweilers were seen by the general public as dogs of terror.

Ironically for us, the role for which we acquired Jack was reversed, and we ended up guarding him for the rest of his life.

When Dale was born, Jack had by now formed a strong bond with us both, and so we took great pains to introduce him carefully to Dale: never ever leaving them alone together. They grew together respectfully. Jack eventually passed away peacefully in my arms at home at nine and a half years old.

The area of garden I had just designed was done simply through explaining my ideas to the customer. Although they were extremely pleased with the end result, I knew I

Dale and Jack share a quiet moment.

needed lots more practical experience, but most importantly, I needed theory in order to express my ideas more fluently and on paper. The six-month course had whetted my appetite and I realised how much there was to learn. So my search began. It wasn't easy because I now had a family to support, so, to begin with, I accepted any work I could get locally, and a series of different jobs followed. This took my total number of jobs since leaving school in 1969 to fifty-two but I did not give up; I knew I would find the right job, and on Monday, 16th January 1989, I began work with a nursery outside Halifax. At last I was enjoying learning in my new career, and bringing home a liveable wage.

Four and a half years went by, and I had become familiar with lots of plant species, learning names and how to care for them, as well as visiting gardens and other nurseries, in-between. During this period, the owner of the nursery had expanded the premises down the lines of a garden centre, to the point where he sold out to a large company. There was no longer the interest in plants there, and I left.

Towards the end of my days at the nursery, they had introduced a dried flower section, for which I was responsible, including ordering and displays. Dried flowers were a relatively new thing and they had really taken off with us, turning over two wagon loads a week. With this in mind, I looked for premises and opened up a shop in Hebden Bridge. Yes, the shop where I began writing this book on the 24th December 1992.

It is now Wednesday, 3rd December 2003. As I mentioned in my introduction, I do not know what will transpire from this writing. Although it has taken me so long to reach this stage, I am ever purposeful, as the years following 1992 have revealed many more reasons why I hope this book may one day fall into the hands of someone who needs strength, encouragement, and above all, faith.

I do hope you have made some sense of my chaotic existence up to now, and that by reading on, you will become as determined in your efforts in life as I am in bringing this book to a present-day conclusion.

"When your efforts come to nothing,
Don't believe it's all in vain,
View every little setback
As a chance to try again.
Forget all thoughts of failure –
That's a word you'll never need,
And take comfort from the knowledge
That you're certain to succeed."
("Don't Give Up" – Anon.)

The cottage at Luddendenfoot provided us with many happy times over the years. It backed on to open countryside, where we took advantage of the steep fields for sledging during the heavy snows of the eighties. We would walk the hillsides, going to bonfires, visiting friends and taking Dale

Dale with Jack 1990.

Me with Dale January 1990. Fields behind our cottage.

The snow of Feb 91! Dale outside our cottage

Outside our cottage Dale. First day at school (Hebden Royd) 21-8-1990

The Cobbles at
Luddenden Foot!
Feb 91.
Sledging with Dale.

Christmas with Dale at
Barkisland

Dale

Feb 91. Dale with Jack down in the woods.

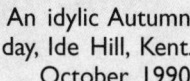

An idylic Autumn day, Ide Hill, Kent. October 1990

117

Dale and Helen
have fun catching
the waves in
Cornwall

Helen, the author
and Dale at a friend's
Wedding 1993

to nursery. There were many holidays to Helen's parents and friends in the South, visiting Wales and Cornwall many times with Dale. Mum would often visit and stay with us, helping Helen with Dale as he grew. She would love to spend Sunday lunch, birthdays and Christmases with us, as Helen always kept a good table, and spoilt mum with her fruitcakes. It was a busy, cosy home and was visited regularly by both Helen's family and mine.

Helen had been working between the chemist's and the health centre throughout these years. The overheads for the shop became too heavy for the takings, so I got a van to travel to customers, selling at the door. But there were several setbacks and the final straw came when we had the van stolen.

With much serious discussion, we both agreed I would go to horticultural college full time for twelve months and finance myself. This was a huge decision for us both, but more so for Helen. We had never been apart. I knew the sacrifices we would both have to make but if, in the long term, it would get me on track to making a stable living and take some pressure off Helen, then it would be worth it. The burning desire within me to design a garden was also becoming difficult to resist.

On Monday, 28th June 1993, I closed the shop.

Following applications to two colleges and much research, I was accepted at Myerscough Agriculture & Horticultural College, Preston, Lancashire, as a mature student. Between then and my enrolment in September, I took two temporary jobs, and on Tuesday, 21st September, aged 39, I enrolled at college for a twelve-month, full-time N.C.H. Landscape Design course.

One of my temporary jobs was at a company hotel from which I was able to get a transfer to a sister hotel near to my college, enabling me to work part-time whilst studying. This all seemed an organised routine, helping me with funds. What I had not realised was how much pressure I had put myself under.

As I embarked on this phase of my life, there was something I knew I just had to come to terms with and put behind me, which had been a burden for me all my life – the fact that I had been rejected by my father.

Back in the early seventies, shortly after I had left school, he just arrived at mum's house one evening, asking if I would sit in his car and have a chat. I was a little nervous, whilst also very pleased that my father wanted to see me. We had had little contact since he and mum had left each other just after I was born.

The half-hour conversation was a little strained, as I had difficulty understanding his broken English. Pressing a ten-pound note firmly into my hand, he asked me to take care of mum, and save my money.

The impact of his sudden visit into my life stirred feelings of wanting to keep in touch with him but he never contacted me again. He told me he had married and now had a boy and a girl and lived in Derbyshire, but that I must never contact him because his wife would not approve.

As I got married and explained this to my wife, there came a point where I felt very strongly that I needed to see him again but after I had made several attempts at visiting him, he told me he did not want to see me anymore. In some ways I felt my father was a coward. He had never told his children that I existed. As I drove home from Derbyshire on that last visit in 1989, the realisation came over me that, to him, I was just a bastard mistake. I began wishing he had never made contact with me. With all the ups and downs with mum over the years, did she feel the same about me?

The only person who gave me love and security was Helen, and in a few hours I would be home. I felt so proud of my wife and son.

Helen was disappointed with the outcome and felt I should now forget my father and move on with my life; which was a positive way of thinking, but only anyone who has experienced being rejected by a parent will know the very deep hurt and emotional impact it has on someone. Unlike bereavement by death, this is someone who is still alive, who has not totally dropped out of your life. This is something you have to learn to live with all through your life. If it has happened in childhood, as it did with me, you carry a question mark around with you, always wondering, why me? This can hold you back with many things in life, and can affect you in such ways as being shy, and lacking in confidence, as in my case. The feeling that a parent does not want you, for me, was demoralising. To grow and have a family of my own was my pride and joy. The difficulty was knowing I had a father who did not want to share that pride and joy. It was like a missing link – a vacuum.

For most of my teenage years, and into my marriage, I would lay the blame for this on mum's doorstep. Often it would crop up in conversation, coming out in anger and bitterness towards mum. Mum has always told me and my brothers and sisters that she has never prevented our fathers from seeing us. Unfortunately for mum, it has taken me many years to realise that whatever the reason for mum and my father parting, he chose to sever all contact with me. Even now, somehow I am always left feeling that I have underachieved, and constantly yearn to do better at whatever it may be that I am trying to be successful at.

This is my way of trying to prove the worthiness of my existence. Something my own father was ashamed of.

Chapter Eleven

The students at college were a mixture of school leavers (most of whom lived in), and mature students, who all travelled each day as they lived close by, except for myself. This meant my lodgings were a two-bedroomed house about a quarter of a mile outside the college, but next door to the college's dairy unit. This environment had a familiarity to it, which was to be appreciated at the end of a stressful day in college.

I was funding myself through college by way of a "Career Development Loan", which was on offer from certain banks at a low interest rate through the college. This was to include college fees and food and lodgings. I had never taken out a loan for anything before. Three thousand pounds was, to say the least, daunting. It had to be justified, and so the heels dug in, and it was nose to the grindstone – not just at college, but evening hotel work as well.

With daily 'phone calls and weekly and fortnightly visits back home for weekends, the family unit, along with Helen's moral support, was helping me cope. The weekends were filled with attention to Dale: taking him to swimming, tennis, gymnastics, and to friends' parties, etc, as well as on many visits to my mum's and Helen's parents at their second home in the next valley. As I mentioned briefly in my introduction, this was a three-storey property, which they had bought shortly after Helen and I had moved from the Golf Club. When they described it to me, I realised it was part of the mill to which I had delivered newspapers in the bottom of the valley, where my auntie had worked.

When I was invited to sleep there it was quite surreal. The huge varnished wooden door, which was the entrance to the office, with its heavily polished brass knob and letterbox where I had posted my papers as a boy, had now gone and had been replaced with a window to the bedroom in which Helen and I were now sleeping. What used to be a thriving family woollen mill had now been converted into a housing complex due to the decline of the woollen industry.

With many college projects behind me, and Christmas approaching, I was looking forward to this time at home with family. We spent Christmas Eve and Christmas Day at Barkisland with Helen's parents and returned home on Boxing Day to spend some time with my family. There were lovely meals and gatherings throughout the Season.

Helen and I had always enjoyed walking, and so continued taking Dale with us whenever we went. A walk through Hardcastle Craggs up to Lumb Falls on the hills above Hebden Bridge completed the Christmas holiday, before my return to college on the 6th January 1994.

We had all been briefed on what work lay ahead in the New Year, and so now the pressure was being felt with the work load leading up to exams which began on 31st January.

The first exam started at 9.30 a.m. – Horticultural Science. I walked up to college from my house as usual. After a heavy shower on the way, blue sky appeared with that feeling that spring was imminent. How could it be, it was still only January? But, apart from it being the only thing that would help to try and take my mind off what was going to happen in the next half an hour, it was a beautiful feeling.

It had not been too bad a winter here, particularly as I was near to the west coast. Helen ("Lainey") had kept me informed of the snow, frost and ice they had been having back at home. However, it had been an extremely wet winter, and now there was every sign that spring was waiting its turn in the role of seasons I so dearly love to keep in touch with. Arriving at college, I made myself scarce, not wanting anyone to realise I was finding it difficult to cope with the situation. First a call to the toilet, then I stood by a radiator to dry my trousers, which had got wet from the shower on my way up to college. As I looked through the window at the queue building up, I tried to condition my mind by telling myself that the others were probably just as nervous, even if they wouldn't admit it. But, with my stomach feeling as though it was in my shoes, I knew I couldn't hide my feelings, and just prayed I could be strong enough to get into the room.

As the queue started to move, I made my way to the end of it, hoping I wouldn't have to speak to anyone. Once inside, we were all allocated seats. Mine was at the very front of the hall on the right-hand side by the windows, which presented me with the most beautiful rays of warm sunshine coming through the windows from the still, clear blue sky, as I looked out through the pine trees in the college grounds.

I felt, for those few moments, such peace and calmness, as the sun warmed my face, as though God was saying, 'You can do it'.

I responded by attempting to read through the exam sheet, which the Adjudicator had already asked us to do. My previous thoughts as I looked out of the window were of the physical "hands-on" side of gardening, which I loved, and of all the other things that went with it, making the outdoors so enjoyable. What was I doing sitting here with this self-inflicted punishment? But I had been calmed by that Presence, and now my thoughts turned to Lainey and Dale. They were the reason I was there.

I had chosen the course knowing my physical capabilities in gardening would be limited in the years ahead in terms of earning a week's wage. Now I had this opportunity, I had to try and deliver the goods, which meant in the form of the exam as well as the rest of the practical course work. As well as Lainey and Dale, I knew I had to prove to myself that, if I did fail the course, it would not be for the want of trying.

At 9.37 a.m. my pen touched the paper with one hour to go. Managing to answer all the questions in some form, right or wrong, at the end I proudly put my two answer sheets together and gathered my coat and bag from the back of the hall to make a swift exit. Once out in the fresh air, with a sigh of relief, I prayed thanks, and told myself I should be able to manage the next four days as I walked back to the college house, appreciative of the outdoors and of the help and support I had from Lainey.

From the day I entered college, I found the most difficult thing to come to terms with was: here I was in a situation at forty years old, akin to that which I found so difficult when I was at school. I kept questioning myself *'why?'* All these years later it was a second chance at education, education for which I felt my brothers and sisters and I had not had full parental support. I can understand you can't make a mathematician out of someone who hasn't got brains, and I never wanted to be one. What I have always felt is that at school I had never had the chance to use the little bit of brain I may possess, in whatever way might have benefited me in later years. That does not mean to say that I did not find happiness once I left school. It is easy to find, and should not be suppressed by anyone.

I knew before I embarked on college that, apart from not being able to afford to continue education after this course, it was as much as I wanted or needed and was capable of. If I could try at this level to gain a qualification, which might make the difference in my being in or out of work in the future, then try I must. Not knowing what work was going to be available even if I gained my qualification added to the strain of going to college.

Lainey had to adjust to being alone for a week or a fortnight at a time: looking after Dale, tending the house, and doing a nearly full-time job.

As I could not obtain a grant from the Council, I was

constantly aware of having to start to pay back the money I had borrowed from the Bank for my course, whether I had passed or failed. Now into the first exams, I knew I could not work any harder at college than I was doing. I am not a natural student, though as long as I continued to put in the effort, pass or fail I knew I should be ready to work at whatever I had to do to provide for us as a family. I had had my second chance, for which I am eternally grateful.

So, as I began to relate to myself again now, after the relief of exams finishing, I was also aware that this was only a temporary freedom of one week, and another six months' college work lay ahead, with yet more exams at the end. I had somehow to stop thinking of it, as I knew it would make it more difficult. *'Just take one day at a time,'* Lainey would say.

With fifteen minutes to go to lunch, I prepared myself for the walk back up to the college canteen. On my way, I enjoyed the same feeling of adrenalin rushing through me that I felt when I started to write this book at Christmas time 1992, fourteen months ago, in my florist shop in Hebden Bridge.

I could not go straight home to Lainey and Dale after the exams because I had to work in the evening at the hotel, where I had part time work whilst at college. This was to pay for the running of my car and any essential expenses. Lainey was holding the fort at home, with her wage being taken up with housekeeping and looking after Dale.

So, with this time between lunch and my evening work, I knew I could continue with my closely guarded secret, my book.

As with nature, I have always had an appreciation of food, no matter how unappetising it may seem sometimes. This I learnt from an early age, both through my experiences at home and with the teaching of my grandparents, who had a high regard for anyone who "licked their platter clean". As I stood in the queue, I could hear disapproving comments about the food from other students. This I found most upsetting, knowing the need that some people have. To my delight, it was oven-baked fish, vegetables and jacket potato; with sweet being a traditional spotted dick made from suet, with white custard. I sat down with my tray and relished it all. It was the first meal I had eaten without feeling nervous since I started college. So much did I enjoy it, that I decided to treat myself by offering to pay for another sweet. The lady serving put her finger to her lips and placed another spotted dick pudding in front of me, and refused the money. This was my little celebration for the last week's work. I returned the empty dish and smiled, giving my thanks as I left the room.

Eager to walk back down to my house, once outside, I looked to the clear blue sky, now with a few sparse clouds racing in the wind, and found myself overcome with emotion from happiness, which I felt was due to a combination of gratitude for the food which I had just received, the relief of exams finishing, being able to continue writing my book from where I had left off over twelve months ago and, above all, because I was going home tomorrow to see Lainey and Dale for over a week during the inter-semester break.

In many ways, I feel a strong person, despite my upbringing. I know I have learned the art of eating well, and to know this does not mean just eating rich and expensive food, but to be aware of, and enjoy, what you are eating whilst you are eating it; whilst in turn, receiving the full nutritional value of every last morsel. I cannot emphasise how much my grandparents played a part in teaching me this. My grandfather was a man who loved his food but would never abuse his body by overeating. I also feel strong because I try to look after my body in terms of health and fitness. Yet, beyond these physical means of well-being, I know that the strongest part of me comes from deep within. This inner strength which I feel keeps me quietly confident as I try to walk the path of life. I can never remember suddenly finding God at any one time in my life, like some people say they have experienced, because I feel I cannot remember a time when I was without Him, or rather when He was not with me. As I mentioned earlier in my book, we were never a strict religious family by means of attending Church regularly but God was always respected in a quiet sort of way within our and my grandparents' home. This was often shown in respecting Sundays by not working, or saying *'thank you'* for our food as we left the table. As I grew through my childhood, I just accepted that God was with me in everything I did, saw and touched, and every day I said my prayers. That is how I grew to know Him through the rest of my life. From a child, growing through into my teens, when I experienced difficult times on the domestic scene, as when I sat in my hen hut in my allotment, and found the load hard to bear, it was as though God was testing me, and building my inner strength. For every difficult experience I came through, He was there waiting for me, turning tears of sadness into tears of joy.

As I still do, I always found happiness from the simplest forms of life. Nature's activity, no matter how small, rarely went unnoticed. Various members of my family would often comment on how sensitive I was, and say how I took things to heart. Whether this was just my natural make-up, or whether it was as a result of my childhood, I do not know. What I do know is, to this day, I have always found the gap between sadness and happiness a very narrow one. As I have grown older, I realise that in the world around us there is lots of both, but find it almost natural whenever having to deal with situations of sadness, because I find it so easy to relate to when I was a child.

There is no doubt in my mind that the main happiness I found as a child was through my grandparents, and as hard as mum tried in her own way, she recognised this and was willing to let me spend whatever time I could with them. Grandad was the world's worst tormentor, and would tease me endlessly, knowing that I loved it. Combined with a strong sense of Yorkshire humour, he had, amongst other things, taught me to laugh at myself. I developed these characteristics, which have helped me to cope with life itself.

My grandfather was the only man I felt I ever really knew whilst growing up. I would follow his every footstep and mimic his mannerisms. I saw him suffer pain through various illnesses; I saw how he mastered the art of walking with only one leg, and how he and my grandmother worked at their marriage for over fifty years. He was in touch with nature and taught me how to stand at the window in their farm cottage and listen to the blackbirds and thrushes singing. I watched closely at how he and my grandmother (nanna) dealt with the situations, however difficult, of their three daughters. Throughout all these observations, I was always aware of grandad's emotions, and of the times when he found words difficult; I could actually see a lump come to his throat as he would fill up, whilst trying to change the subject.

The gap between losing my grandfather and my later years has often presented me with the question of how men cope with their emotions. I would find it difficult if I even dared to ask any man if he ever cried, to admit that he did; although I am sure most men at some time in their life feel like crying. It is most likely done behind closed doors, and never spoken of because it may appear a weakness in them as men. The difficulty comes through men feeling they have to give the image in life that they are stronger than women. This, I'm sure, is true in most physical cases but becomes a barrier when trying to deal with their emotions.

So, do some men actually never cry? I only know that for me, besides my physical strength, I have found that crying has built me an inner strength which I have needed to carry me through difficult times over the years. The strangest thing I find is that I also cry when I am most happy. I almost see sadness and happiness as a form of symbiosis in life's intricate pattern, which may be the reason for the narrow gap I have always found between them. I often thought, as I grew older, some form of metamorphosis would reduce my ability to cry. Had I not cried as much as a child, maybe the gap would have been bigger.

Of course, my periods of happiness over the years have increased, both with my own efforts and, since I got married, through my wife and my son. It is up to me now to ensure those periods continue, making that gap even bigger for Dale's future.

It is in the hope that, by revealing how I deal with my emotions, this also may be a help to anyone reading this book who may question themselves at some point in their life. Whether experienced by man or woman, I have grown to realise that crying is nothing to be ashamed of and, for whatever reason – sadness or happiness – it leaves behind that natural inner strength.

Friday, 4th February 1994 – 10.30 a.m. As I came out of the exam room, I recalled my immediate feeling of not wanting to speak to anyone, feeling almost stunned by the sudden end to the climax of a week of exams. I stopped just out of the college gate, zipping my Barbour, which had protected me from the elements over the last four and a half months. The wind blew strongly, as if to greet me, and welcome me back to my great outdoors; I had been stifled by a classroom situation for those past months. Though it was a strong wind, it did not convey to me the wildness and presence of nature which I felt so strongly in the wind on the Pennine Valleys across the border in my Yorkshire. Oblivious to anyone around me, I walked into the wind submissively, prepared for it to transport me like a pollen grain back to my own species of plant survivors that grow in the wild, as opposed to the cultivars grown by man, which would die out if left.

Halfway down the lane, as I looked up towards the strong winter sun beaming down, as it had on alternate days through exam week, there in the clear blue sky, riding the wind, was a lone seagull. It was so reminiscent of the one my wife had pointed out to me on a similar day whilst walking in Yorkshire when we were courting some thirteen years ago. I couldn't understand why she referred to it as *"Jonathan Livingstone Seagull"*, until she gave me a book to read by this title; a story of which I became very fond.

On arriving back at my room, the file containing all my past notes lay on my desk at the bottom of my bed, just as I had left it two hours ago, after one last attempt at quick revision. I promptly closed it, confirming to myself that the hard core of theory was now all behind me, and took satisfaction from the fact that even though I did not and would not know my results for a few weeks, I had tried.

At this point, my whole body slumped into the chair as tears flowed and I made no effort to hold them back. I was mentally drained. I know some students, particularly the younger ones, did not find studying too difficult, and I found them quite supportive towards me, but I am not an academic, and I just hoped and prayed that my one hundred per cent effort would reward me with, at least, a pass grade.

There is something in me that makes me so determined to succeed at whatever goal I set myself in life. It is almost a way of proving myself and constantly trying to catch up with what I missed out on in my childhood. Along with this feeling is the very fact that if I could succeed that meant I would have to punish myself in some way, usually by taking the hardest route to gain any success. This, in turn, makes me feel worthy of anything I achieve in life. One thing, of which I am sure, is the combination of my upbringing and being a Yorkshire man is responsible for my approach to life. It could be argued that it is because my birth sign is Taurus but I do not understand the stars, so I am inclined to let that matter ride.

My punishment for my goal at the time was having to be away from my wife and son, and work in a way I was not used to for twelve months in order to achieve my goal. It may be said that this was my decision and my wife was also suffering by not having her husband at home. Something I have always been aware of in marriage is compromise, and I must say at this stage that Lainey was much better at it than I was. However, with such decisions as the college course, it was a true compromise, whilst we both knew how difficult work was becoming for me.

Since getting married, like most people I have had to change my type of goals in life, though Lainey very rarely opposes anything I decide to do and, to the contrary, gives me one hundred per cent support. When embarking on these goals, my aim is to provide a better quality of life. Before I was married, it was for me; it is now for us as a family, in the hope that Dale will have a better start to life than I had. When I was single, although like most young people I felt I could reach for the moon, I was always realistic as to the goals I set myself, relating to my capabilities and what I could afford. Now, with a family to support, I find it increasingly difficult to adhere to this approach, as the financial pressures of life quite often result in Hobson's choice. Even so, however difficult times become, whatever path I take, I have to believe in myself, if now not for my sake, then for Lainey and Dale's.

Saturday, 5th February 1994 – the day after finishing my exams. I had had two good days writing this book, and had packed up before going to my evening work at the hotel, after which, at 11.00 p.m. I began my journey home to Lainey and Dale, and of course, Yorkshire.

Dale was beginning to show an interest in helping me with jobs around the garden, which I would take on whilst at home. Feeding his pet rabbit "Bramble" and watching the doves which we had, I hoped would introduce him to nature. He had begun asking me things about plants, and became very proud of himself by being able to recall the name "Urtica Dioica" – Latin for "nettle". He was the apple of my eye. Those weekends meant so much to me, but studying was heavy now, which meant I was unable to come home as often in the weekends ahead.

Some time into March, on one of my visits home, I was aware of a sudden coldness from Lainey towards me. There would be less effort at mealtimes, and less conversation. She would read a book in bed. I knew something was wrong but did not know how to approach her; she seemed to have changed and become silent, with a rejection towards me. She was now spending most of her time at Barkisland with Dale and her parents. I understood how difficult it must be for her but felt helpless to do anything at this stage, and hoped that things would adjust once I finished college in July.

Friday, 25th March 1994 – 4.15 p.m. back at college. As I lay on top of my bed, my head towards the bottom, so as to bask in the clear, sparkling sunshine which forced itself upon me, I inhaled the fresh, cool spring air that I had welcomed into my room by opening the window next to my bed a couple of hours before.

I had settled myself with a book I had chosen from the college library some weeks ago on a landscape designer – "Lanning Roper and his Gardens" by Jane Brown. Although we had been briefed on other more prominent designers, as this was an assignment for our course work, I was immediately captivated by this book about a designer I had never heard mentioned. After reading the first page of her introduction, I booked it out, and due to the volume of other college work found great frustration in being unable to read it until now. Into the fourth page of the introduction I was so moved I did not want to stop reading it, and realised that I was studying what I felt so passionate about and what made me so very happy deep within.

As a ray of sun caught my eye, I looked out to the clear blue spring sky through the silhouette of a still leafless tree, which blurred with the sunshine as unrestrained tears emerged. I had to go to work in a couple of hours at my evening employment, which I had endured for the last six months, at a hotel which was in turmoil with staffing problems. Yet again, I was unable to go home after college had finished, as the Friday evening, and all day the following Saturday would earn me £30.00 at the hotel, which was going to be well short of what was needed to contribute towards Lainey's housekeeping, my petrol, the college fees and Dale's birthday which was approaching.

I was counting the weeks now to the end of the course and knew that I must use some of the time over the Easter holidays to seek some kind of employment. Though the horticultural journals had a reasonable amount of vacancies, and the industry was still enjoying growth despite the effects of the last five years' recession, I knew that there was little work in the valley back home.

The strain of being away from Lainey and Dale for such long periods had taken its toll on us both, and I knew we would all need to readjust after my being away. The thought of being unable to work at what I had been studying for the last twelve months was daunting. Whether I qualified at college or not, horticulture had made its impression on me over the years, and I now felt I had sufficient knowledge to work at it in a more professional capacity.

Saturday morning I woke at 9.30 a.m., drew back my curtains, and opened the window to the most beautiful, warm, sunny day, quite unusual for March. I put my dressing gown on and leaned out of the window, saying my prayers of thanks as I observed flora and fauna, whilst in turn, for those few minutes, my whole being was filled with peace. Those few minutes helped prepare me for the day ahead at the hotel, as well as telling me that the new life that spring was bringing forth would keep me strong and everything was going to be alright.

The three weeks' semester break leading up to 18th April gave us all plenty of time together. There was the usual toing and froing to Barkisland and my mum's, as well as joining Lainey's parents with friends for day trips. I was also able to complete landscaping the next-door neighbour's garden, which I had begun on previous weekends. This had brought us in some extra cash. But, throughout this time, as hard as I tried, I knew Lainey and I were just not connecting.

A week later I was home for Dale's birthday. I completed icing his cake, which Lainey had made, along with arranging for his friends to join him. We all had a lovely day tenpin bowling, before I had to return to college.

By now, I was feeling completely out in the cold with Lainey's attitude towards me. The hotel work had become too stressful, as I worked late into the evenings after studies, but before I left I managed to get a part-time job at a nursery close to the college, which was ideal.

Sunday, 24th April 1994 – 6.30 p.m. Whilst studying "Lanning Roper and his Gardens", I heard the first rumble of this year's thunder. As I rose to open my bedroom window, I viewed the dramatic contrast of clear purple/slate grey sky against circling pure white cotton-like clouds that was preparing us for a thunderstorm. But as the loud claps of thunder became more distant, light blue patches broke in the sky, whilst at the same time rain fell gently on this year's new growth as I realised a heavy downpour was being delivered in another area.

The fresh air now blowing through the window was yet again to heighten my sense of old Mother Nature! She made me feel so comfortable and secure as she reminded me she was still in control, presenting us with unlimited shades of lush green. This was a welcome reminder that summer was imminent, and this time was to be enjoyed as much as the beautiful colours and fragrances which would follow when the British Summer was in its glory. I took a deep breath and returned to Jane Brown's "Lanning Roper and his Gardens".

There were few weekends now when I could get home as the work increased towards the final exams. I was also making endless applications for jobs. Replacing my home visits with telephone calls was heart wrenching, as Lainey would withhold any of the happenings at home, and keep our conversation short. I would leave the telephone with mixed feelings about the journey on which I had embarked, wondering what the future would hold.

On 4th July we began our final exams, and completed them on the 7th. I had two days' work to complete at the nursery, which meant staying on until the Saturday. On Saturday, 9th July 1994 I handed my house keys in to the college and drove away, feeling total relief and elation, even though at this stage I was unaware of my results.

Chapter Twelve

Whatever difficulties I have been presented with through my life, I have always remained positive through prayer. I would never challenge anyone to prove or disprove whether or not there is a god. I use the name "God" in prayer purely because I grew to know that name as a child. I am not ashamed of the fact that my knowledge of the Bible is almost nil. What I do know is, I have never needed a book to work out why or to whom I am praying. I have always felt a very strong spiritual presence, which I believe we can all respond to if we wish. It is not easy for any of us to accept everything that happens in our lives, but one thing I know for certain, and that is, as much as some would like to think we are, we are not always in control. For me this has become more so since I have grown older; when such times have presented themselves, my spiritual awareness has deepened, and never more than during the next three years of my life.

Change is something we can all usually accept easily if we ourselves are making the change, which, in turn, makes us feel in control. Though when we are on the receiving end of change it can be very difficult to accept, as we then feel out of control. I must point out at this stage that I am not trying to theorise, but from my own experience, when I have found certain change difficult, my prayers have helped me, even if only slowly, to embrace that change rather than obstinately to resist it. I do believe that, if we can learn to do this, then spiritually we are allowed to grow and move on with our lives. By observing this, I have noticed people, including myself if I look back, who when they have resisted it, have just simply stood still with their lives. I am sure we can all relate to a time when we have felt out of control. There is a reason for change, and it is out of our control.

In 1995 I found such a time extremely difficult to deal with, but fate stepped in, and eventually I was once again able to embrace change.

The day after I finished college, mum took Lainey and me to buy us a dining table as a present to celebrate my having completed college, and I think possibly in sympathy for the hardship Lainey had been through. A couple of weeks later, Lainey's parents treated us to a two-week summer holiday in Cornwall. In the meantime, I was making literally dozens of applications for work relating to my college course.

Once back from our holidays, the pressure was on for me to find work, and I realised I was going to have to accept anything that would bring a wage home, so I did; yet again, a series of jobs followed but also, unfortunately, so did a change in my character, which I could never have believed or understood, had I not come through the other side of the longest, darkest tunnel I have been through. Only years later, looking back, was I able to see, understand, and accept for myself that I had plummeted into a deep depression. Although family and friends recognised it and pointed it out to me, sadly, at the time, I did not, and instead became angry and I would think now looking back, unbearable to live with.

The small cottage we lived in seemed to become smaller by the day, as everything began to close in on me. Each time, as I appeared through the door after searching for the kind of work with which I had dreamed my college studies would reward me, the desperate expression on my face would reflect in total sadness on Lainey's, which made me feel so guilty and, in turn, angry that the atmosphere became so tense that we dared not speak to one another. Some evenings I would leave the cottage in silence and walk for miles around the tops of the valley and even, on occasions, would not return home until the early hours of the following morning, after sitting in derelict barns, half falling asleep whilst trying to pray, wondering how I could get my family out of this terrible mess. But there did not seem to be any answer. Only such a very strong feeling and force within me that I knew I would one day find my dream. But how does one manage to convince one's wife, who is under pressure bringing up a child, that one will succeed? In my case, I couldn't.

On the 11th February 1995, Lainey told me she was possibly leaving. I was trying so hard to go through the motions of family life that it did not register, and possibly I did not want to hear what she had said. At this point I was working for a local firm which itself was struggling to find work. The recession had affected most of the country by now and I was desperate for us to move out of the valley, as I knew the type of work I was aiming for was out there somewhere. But Lainey did not want to move; she had lost all confidence in me.

One morning, as Lainey was preparing for work, she was trying to encourage me to be positive. I had got out of bed and was wearing my dressing gown. Things were bad; I had no answers for her, only a blank, vacant expression which I did not want the rest of the world to see.

Minutes after Lainey left, I locked the door and drew the lounge curtains. Then, looking up at the landing spindles at the top of the stairs, removed my dressing gown belt and tied it round one of the spindles. From that moment everything went blank. Then, suddenly there was an anxious knocking at the door. It startled me. I quickly removed my belt from the spindle and opened the door. It was Lainey. Her expression and tone of voice were a mixture of annoyance and concern as she enquired why the curtains were drawn. She had seen them as she was driving on the main road below and came back. I can't recall my exact answer, except I know it was a feeble excuse, and I wonder to this day if she ever suspected my intentions.

After Lainey left, I was stunned for a while. I was frightened at the realisation of my intentions, whilst at the same time angry with myself that I had caused Lainey so much concern. I knew fate had stepped in. Although Lainey had said very little before she left, I felt as though I had been scolded by someone. As I stood calmly on the landing, I could hear an inner voice telling me to move on. That was my turning point. I owed it to everyone who had been trying to help me, to help myself. It was as though I had taken a wrong turning and couldn't find my way back. I had simply got lost in life, and needed time to get back on the path.

That sounds very easy to say now, but going through that period was far from simple. There were more questions than answers. It was now a slow process of conditioning myself with positive thoughts. I had always loved life, and I would continue to do so, along with Lainey and Dale. The quotation, *"There is no gain without pain"* is one I have often heard, and always thought sounded very unfair, but now I was to realise how poignant it would be to me.

Like picking out stepping-stones whilst trying to cross a fast running stream, I slipped from one job to another in the valley, none of them sound, because the firms themselves found difficulty in employing anyone as the recession plunged deeper. Including my college course and part-time work whilst studying, my job total since leaving school had now reached sixty-two!

I tried further afield and applied to the pest control firm "Rentokil", which had a vacancy in its plant interior division based at the far side of Leeds. This meant an hour's journey to and from work but I was desperate and took the job, starting on Monday, 3rd April 1995. That evening, as I came home, Lainey told me again that she wanted to leave me. This time I was scared, unable to reason about or to justify our future, as she chose to stay silent and focus on Dale.

The following weekend, I took Lainey and Dale to the

National Railway Museum at York. Little did I know that was to be our last day out together as a family. Her parents were up from London, staying at Barkisland for Easter. During the week, as Dale had broken up from school, Lainey and her parents had arranged for him to stay there. I was to come to realise why.

On Thursday, 13th April 1995, as I returned home from work, Lainey told me she was leaving that night, and if I wanted to I could go with her to Barkisland to see Dale. I jolted on the chair, unable to prepare myself for this. A deep sickly feeling came over me. She calmly, with no emotion, led me to the car. It all felt so unreal, my legs felt they would let me down before I got to the car. Once seated inside, I pleaded with her not to go through with this, but it was as though she was on automatic pilot; I could not connect with her.

The drive to Barkisland was agonising. Somehow I managed to contain myself so as not to cause any trauma for Dale. As we stepped inside the house, Helen's parents stood in front of me with little to say. I knelt down in front of Dale and tried to assure him that I would see him soon without making too big an issue for him – he would be eight years old in a week's time. His face was solemn; I knew he could sense there was something wrong. I felt glued to the floor as I rested both hands on his shoulders. The tears finally came, and with my head bowed in humiliation, I stood up and turned to leave.

Since losing my grandfather, this was the worst moment of my life. I heard Lainey offer me a lift home, which I refused as I walked outside. It was dark, I cannot remember the time. I tried to be strong enough to walk the five miles home, but once up into the village shock got the better of me, as I broke down on the roadside. I recall finding a 'phone box and contacting mum, who arranged for my two sisters to come and pick me up.

Days, weeks and months later, ever hopeful, I had discussions with Lainey, hoping she would consider us having a fresh start, but it was as though I could not get through. There seemed to be something she wasn't telling me. I wondered if her parents had influenced her to leave me; she was very close to her pa. After several attempts at asking her why she had left, her only answer was – *'Lots of little things'*.

Dale was now becoming my primary concern. For some reason, Lainey never took court action for custody of Dale, for which I was so grateful. So he was allowed to see me whenever he wished. Although I made great efforts to spend as much time as possible with him, I was very conscious not to put pressure on him to visit me, as I was unsure of how much Dale was involved in our separation. Then, one Sunday evening in August that year, Lainey came to collect Dale at 5.00 p.m. As she stood at the door I could see she was upset, so I asked her in. She said she had something to tell me. We both went into Dale's bedroom whilst Dale was entertained by mum and some friends downstairs. Her next words were, *'I've been seeing someone.'* I recall a feeling of confusion, wondering if she was trying to taunt me with her actions, whilst at the same time thinking I could detect a hint of regret in what she was saying. My immediate reaction was not of anger, but strangely enough, more of relief that my earlier suspicions were not unfounded.

On Lainey's next visit I drew strength to ask a question I knew would be extremely painful to us both – had they become intimate? She answered, *'Yes'*. I felt the final nail in the coffin as I opened the door and asked her to leave. The following moments left me filled with anger. Hands clasped, I prayed for composure, my love of life would continue, although Lainey had chosen not to share it with me. As for Dale, only time would tell. He had a lot of growing to do and would make his own mind up about things. My concern was that he should be affected as little as possible by our parting.

For myself, pursuing my dream was going to be a lonely affair. Why should there be "no gain without pain"? It seems so very unfair.

"If you are true to your own vision
You will triumph over all odds."

So, I will now go forward, albeit through the face of adversity.

It is at this stage in my life, and as I write, that I may deeply encourage and give hope to anyone who may be unfortunate to be in such a desperate time of their life, to go forward with prayer.

Chapter Thirteen

By now, weekends were all I lived for. Dale had half a dozen or so friends he had grown up with through nursery, infant and junior school. So most weekends were spent taking him to parties and friends' outings. As a family we would invite his friends to our cottage. Lainey was a good host, and took special delight in having all the children there. We would relish listening to their laughter and watching their antics, whilst making sure they were all fed and watered before leaving. So I would make sure that continued for Dale. It was vitally important for his stability to try and keep his routine, however difficult it proved for me.

Only a few months ago I had been a husband and father, a role into which I had grown over the last fourteen years. The impact of having that suddenly taken away had shaken my foundations. Walking into an empty house each night from work now left me wondering where I fitted in to life. It was not easy trying to get used to being a part-time dad.

Each time Dale left at weekends the prospect of another whole week alone was daunting. This was a situation totally out of my control: a change – a change that would test me to the limits. How could I possibly embrace this change?

The childhood I had grown up with had left me able to cope domestically. There was much welcome support from a few close friends by way of telephone calls and encouragement and, of course, the unfailing support and love only a mum could provide. As you will recall from my mentioning earlier in the book, mum had certainly found it difficult to let us go from the nest, causing me much pain at times when I was experiencing happiness but, should any of us find ourselves in difficulty, she would go to extraordinary lengths to ensure our well-being. None more so than now: helping me to survive a failed marriage.

The interior landscaping work was taking me as far afield as Newcastle, The Borders, Liverpool and Wales. Since Lainey and Dale had left, trying to get through my domestic chores of keeping the house clean after arriving home late in the evenings from work, as well as preparing for Dale and his friends at weekends, was leaving me exhausted. At some point every single day since Lainey and Dale had left I cried. This continued for two years. It was when I was driving home in rush hour traffic from work one evening to meet Dale that I realised I was losing my confidence on the road. Everything was suddenly spiralling out of control. There were bills I was finding difficult to pay, house chores building up, etc. Eventually, I gave way to pride and made a visit to the doctor, who put me on a course of tablets to calm me. To my horror, he gave me a sick note for work, advising me to stop driving for a couple of weeks. I knew it was the sensible thing to do, so took his advice.

I will never forget to this day the quietly-spoken lady who, when I walked into the Citizens' Advice Bureau in Hebden Bridge, and presented her with a carrier bag full of bills and legal correspondence, unburdened me with a few words of reassurance. This was followed up in the weeks ahead by her successful voluntary help. I am forever grateful.

It is so easy to forget how fragile our lives are, and the friendships and relationships that run alongside them. People drop in and out of our lives as we weave our way through, some staying longer than others, but all playing their part in life's intricate pattern. Someone once told me that, if we can count on one hand the number of true friends we have in our lifetime, we are very lucky. During our time at the Golf Club back in 1982–84, I found a small pet shop in Hebden Bridge, where I began to get our dog Jack's food and supplies. The owners had just taken over the business, which had been very badly run-down. I came to know them as Rita and Gordon, and we have remained friends ever since.

The strain of Lainey and Dale leaving was not allowing me to concentrate on my new direction, and I felt I needed something very low key until I began to feel strong enough to move forward. Rita and Gordon offered me temporary work at the pet shop. This was a great help and, although it meant I was living on a shoestring after giving up with the interior landscaping, it was all I could manage mentally and physically at that time. This was rock bottom. I was unable to afford to run the small car I had, which was now beyond repair. But, there was still Shanks's pony, and the walks along the canal to work were good for the soul.

Although it was only a small circle of people Lainey and I knew through Dale's friends and locals, when they suddenly stopped visiting due to our circumstances, a feeling of isolation began to creep in. It was now that I came to know what a true friend was. I was extremely sensitive as to how people reacted when they found out about our situation, and became almost defensive towards Lainey, so as not to hear anyone speak against her. Had our past relationship not been as strong, maybe I would have felt differently, but we were both responsible for the outcome. Rita and Gordon were good listeners, and did not take sides, which made it easy for me to unburden myself. In those early days I would stay with them into the early hours before returning to the empty cottage. They would treat me to evening meals at our favourite country haunts around the valley after they closed the shop, and on occasions I would have them over for homemade supper.

Although people kept saying that Lainey would be considering divorce proceedings, I was trying to shut this out of my mind. When eventually she mentioned it to me, we both agreed to wait the two years required for it to go through automatically. Apparently, this was to save either of us blaming the other, which would have meant earlier proceedings but with more distress.

During those two years I never gave up hope, but made a feeble attempt at living one day at a time, gradually withdrawing into myself. The 'phone calls I received from Tony in the Lakes and Jan up in Newcastle, along with the support from one of my sisters and mum, was all I had to cling onto when Dale was not there.

Mum thought very dearly of Dale. She had helped Lainey with him as a baby, drawing on all her own experience with us over the years. Lainey was grateful for this when her parents were so far away in London. I could see the sympathy mum had for Dale's situation now, along with the hurt she was feeling for me. Now that she was in her late sixties I was concerned when she walked up the valley side in all weathers with food supplies, and helped to keep the cottage and garden tidy. I could not let this carry on. I had to begin to stand alone in life. Therefore I asked mum and my sister Sandra to give me some time alone now, which, looking back, mum must have found upsetting. She still had to divide her time between my other brothers and sisters, which I felt only fair.

Towards the end of that year (1995), Dale had spent few weekends with me, as he was away in London some of the time. There had been a heavy snowfall over the weekend of 10th December and I took him snowballing. That was the last contact Lainey and Dale made with me that year.

In November I had taken some restaurant work at a local old country house hotel I had known of previously, in order to keep the wolf from the door, and to buy Christmas presents. I felt like two different people as, digging out my old tuxedo, I immersed myself in the season's festivities, working into the small hours, serving all the rich and exotic fare the elite would expect in such an establishment. At first it was like putting old slippers on, but as Christmas drew nearer, the hours got longer. The standard and attention to customers was no less than impeccable. This was a very busy family-run hotel. Service was stressful, enduring endless silver flats from the heat of the kitchen to the decibels of live music and excited punters. By the end of my shift I would be able to wring my shirt out, as sweat had oozed from every part of my body. I would then man the bar.

As I stood, after bar duties, savouring the sudden quiet, I looked through the leaded mullion windows as a gentle covering of snow lit up the garden. I longed to touch the grey winter foliage surrounding the hotels parterre. The cool winter's air would be welcoming after the smoke-filled air left in the bar by customers' cigars. But the 'phone rang for continuing duties, and my role as waiter went on until early next morning. Once home, I locked the door and returned to my isolation.

I had continued all year posting applications for horticultural positions, but with no success. Until one morning late in December the 'phone rang. A very positive lady's voice enquired at the other end, *'Do you want a job?'* Then apologising for not replying earlier, she told me that she had been in Vienna since November and had just found my letter behind the door when she arrived back yesterday. She introduced herself to me as *'Mrs ?'*. I had replied to a box number given in an advertisement four weeks ago in the *Halifax Evening Courier* for the position of gardener at a private house. An interview was arranged for Sunday, 24th December 1995 at 10.30 a.m., after which Mrs ? gave me directions.

I can remember putting the 'phone down and trying to stop myself becoming excited. Could this be a breakthrough to what I had been searching for? Or, better still, should I even dare to think – could it <u>be</u> what I had been searching for? Although there was no one else in the house, I afforded myself a smile as I drew back the bedroom curtains; then remained quietly confident until the interview.

A couple of hundred yards off the main road, through a lodge gate bearing the sign "Kingston", I turned into a drive. The gravel crunched under my tyres, giving that sound I had often heard on television when cars did this in films. As I turned into the circle, a grand solidly-built stone house stood in front of me in its own grounds. There was much noise from dogs barking. Then, from behind a pair of large wooden gates, peered a man with glasses and casual clothes and, as though I was unexpected, he wore an inquisitive frown which gradually broke into a smile. With a Pekingese under one arm, and two more at his feet, along with a golden retriever, he opened the gate and greeted me. This was the rear entrance to the house. He asked me to wait in the yard until he informed Mrs ? of my arrival.

On returning, he had been instructed to give me a tour of the grounds, during which time he introduced himself to me as Adrian. Adrian explained his duties to me; they were those of a butler-cum-housemaid-cum-gardener-cum-handyman. This, I thought, would probably explain his very untidy appearance, but I was later to find out otherwise. The grounds were very formally laid out and reasonably tidy, though the soil, and the grounds as a whole, looked very tired.

Adrian was a heavyweight, though not very tall. As he briefed me on my duties and the general running of the place by himself and other staff, his shoulders bounced up and down and he broke into a chesty laugh, exposing numerous decayed teeth. This was due to the astonished expression on my face, which I was to find out later he had witnessed on many other applicants' faces.

Returning to the yard, he ushered me into the potting shed, where he asked me to wait until Mrs. ? arrived. I pondered over the immaculate whitewashed walls, where all the old garden tools hung in their rightful places. A small stove burnt steadily, barely giving off any heat. Moments later the door opened, and in walked, or rather stooped, a strong determined figure with a facial expression to match. In the corner, behind the door, was a wooden coal bunker with a simple seat attached, which I offered her. She declined in a very proud manner, and turned to face me as she made a conscious effort to correct her stoop. Her attire was immaculate, as she boasted a black and yellow tartan dress with black velvet bib, and a choice brooch. But my eyes found it difficult to stop focusing on her hair, which was bluer than blue with not a hair out of place – obviously from a recent hair appointment. But her eyes looked glazed behind her glasses as she asked me, *'What can you do?'* Whilst I was delivering my answer, she gave way to a smile that seemed as though it had been forgotten for years.

A wage was agreed, and her eagerness for me to start the following morning would have been welcomed had I not had to work two weeks' notice at the hotel. So we agreed that I would begin work on Monday, 8th January 1996 – what a beautiful Christmas present.

A few days before, I had found Christmas cards and a present from Dale in my outside postbox: they had been left whilst I was out. Tomorrow was Christmas Day, and they had not arranged for Dale to be with me over Christmas, so I knew I had to get a grip of myself and keep busy. If ever there was a time that a man could be destroyed, this was it. I knew I must take heed of others now and keep myself busy, so I accepted working Christmas Day lunch at the hotel.

I awoke to the alarm at 8.45 a.m. As I slowly became aware that it was Christmas Day, I could feel myself taken into a trancelike state, my mind finding it difficult to function, knowing I had to try and get through this day with more than a smile. – Dare I move? Was it real? Were my wife and son really not here to share all the simple family activities which helped to release so much love? I pulled the top flannelette sheet closer to my chin for a few more minutes' comfort, but then suddenly realised that there was a warmth I had not felt in two weeks, since I last saw Dale. I had put the central heating on the night before and the very hard frost that came that night had softened me enough to leave it on all night, with the thought that I would now be able to start the New Year with a full-time job.

So, hard as I tried to condition my mind, as I opened the bedroom door to go into the bathroom, I hesitated by Dale's bedroom door, and the tears broke through. Was I going to lose my battle for a day's work to pay for the winter bills? I shouted something loud enough to shock myself and continued into the bathroom whilst listening to the morning service on the wireless. Everything they played: carols, sermons, seemed so poignant, making it even harder to get through the day ahead. Once dressed, I took a few quiet moments at the foot of our bed to say my prayers.

Although Dale's rabbits, which had been left with me, were a bit of a financial drain, being living things they gave me a purpose and, above all, were the last link with Dale. As I opened the porch door to go and clean them out and feed them, I braced myself as the air from the thick, glistening frost cut into me. The valley was quiet, and as I looked around, I wondered who would be the first person I could wish merry Christmas to. Well, it didn't have to be a person did it? So, as I put the chopped veg and breadcrumbs on the bird table, my first Christmas wishes went out to the birds and then to the rabbits. For all my sadness, I feel so privileged that my affinity with nature is my given strength, and I absorbed all she had on offer in the few minutes I had in the garden before driving to the hotel to carry out my role as restaurant waiter.

As I entered the restaurant at 11.35 a.m., muffled with scarf and coat, I will never forget the few minutes that followed for the rest of my life. A waiter, three waitresses, the restaurant manager and the manager stood casually chatting and were apparently waiting for me to make up the final member of staff for Christmas lunch service. As I exchanged Christmas greetings, there was a feeling of half-heartedness. Did it show on my face that I was carrying a burden, which I tried so hard to conceal? The expressions which each face revealed were of rather being with their loved ones at this family time than working. However, like myself, they had taken the carrot on offer – triple pay (£9.00 per hour) – no doubt they were as needy as me.

Then came the numbness, followed by nerves. The manager announced his brief as usual. As he began, I was taking in the atmosphere of the 16th century restaurant, with its three cosy individual rooms, log fires and tartan Christmas crackers, hoping the hustle and bustle would take my mind off my personal circumstances and carry me through the next few hours, when I heard, *'Stephen! You will be serving the family upstairs by yourself.'* 'The family' being: the two sisters, owners of the hotel, and their husbands and children. *'They are to have champagne and canapés on arrival at 12.30 p.m.'* After his instructions to me, almost as though he sensed I had a problem, he finished by saying, *'Alright?'* I did not hesitate in saying, *'Yes'*, but the second after knew that, in all my nearly twenty years of catering experience, during which I had served some quite important guests, I had never felt as nervous and alone as then.

I waited for the completion of his brief to the rest of the staff, and then made my way upstairs into what used to be the family's bedrooms, where one was being used as Reception Lounge for their champagne arrival. I took a few minutes to gather and compose myself, looking out through the leaded stone mullioned windows. The light snowfall from the night before was enough to capture the traditional Christmas scene, which so befitted this old house at this time of year. The view was over the front entrance, taking in a couple of weeping willows and the footpath, which led from two huge stone pillars, each supporting a ball finial. These scaled up from the weeping willows to cedars and pines beyond, which completed the overall setting. They enclosed a circular driveway and I could almost hear the sound of coach and horses drawing up to be attended by the footman.

Rightly or wrongly, I felt a sense of worthiness that I had been chosen to serve the family, and hoped my sadness would allow me to carry it through, so as at least to see someone have a happy Christmas, which was what I was so desperate for. At that moment, my thoughts were broken as one of the sisters breezed into the room and wished me 'Happy Christmas!' As I returned her greetings, the rest of the family arrived and I began my duties.

Although, years ago, I had had the pleasure of being employed temporarily by the daughter's parents, I had never been in contact with the two daughters, though I found them quite friendly and comfortable to serve at the table. By the time they had completed their six courses and nine bottles of wine, the party of sixteen were very relaxed. Five o'clock saw them departing and I began to clear the room of debris from crackers, etc. Although I knew I had made every effort in my work of service to the family, my underlying thought was – were they happy? I had taken some glasses downstairs to the Bar and, on returning, I was met by the husband of one of the sisters. As he looked at me, he gave a nod of approval with some words of thanks and placed two £20.00 notes into my right hand. My immediate response was to say 'Thank you', which I almost felt should have been accompanied by bended knees such was my financial strain at home. However, I knew the rules and policies of the management, and with all loyalty, handed the £40.00 to the Italian restaurant manager, and never saw a penny of it again.

I was very much aware of these happenings in the industry, and when, in 1980, I eventually held the position of restaurant manager in a small family-run country hotel in the Yorkshire Dales, I took great pleasure in seeing the delight on the faces of my staff when I shared out their hard-earned tips at the end of the week, which they had not received from the previous manager. Maybe if I had not done this, I could have had a more comfortable living but, when someone comes up with the goods, I believe in reward, and to this day, the satisfaction of being able to reward someone for their efforts is what keeps me striving in my own efforts.

I had not only got stuck on climbing the ladder in life, but somehow, at the age of forty had slipped back to the bottom, with quite a few bruises. One has to realise that I was scratching a living as a part-time waiter at £3.00 per hour. Much more painful than the bruises was the open wound I was nursing at that time, which was the breakdown of my own family, and the feeling of being a failure.

There was no Christmas meal for any of the staff after work had finished, and everyone was attending to last minute tidying up. At one point, nearing the end of food service, I had to go down into the wine cellar for one last bottle for the family. During those few seconds a voice called out my name; it was the head chef. I replied and looked up to see him standing beside me, enquiring if I would like a piece of Christmas pud to take home. I'm not sure what the expression on my face revealed to him, but astonished, I eventually replied how kind his offer was, only for him to return seconds later, placing a whole Christmas pudding, carefully wrapped, and announcing it was for me. Although I prefer to give than receive, I know what pleasure can be gained when something is gratefully received, and so hope that I gave the Chef that pleasure. It was the first year that I had never had any Christmas pudding, Christmas cake or other Christmas food in the house, but my willpower was strong enough to put the Christmas pudding in the freezer, where I would treasure it until, hopefully, a special occasion should come along.

At 5.30 p.m. I signed off my shift, said my goodbyes and headed home. My driving was uneasy as I thought of how Lainey and Dale might be spending Christmas Day. Was I simply just not in their thoughts? I realised that I should stop this incessant questioning of myself and just get on with life, but it seemed so selfish to get on with life when I could not share it with the ones I loved. I arrived home. After much pushing and shoving I managed to get the swollen wooden door to open. I remembered how Lainey found it almost impossible to deal with at this time of year: just one of the many things that must have caused her to leave.

Once inside, I drew the velvet curtain behind the door, hoping it would help to retain some of the warmth from the central heating, which I had been forced to put on due to the below zero temperatures. There were baked beans and sweet corn in the fridge; it was easy to warm them in the saucepan and open a tin of sardines. I was so tired. I placed my meal on the table, sat down, and whilst feeling quite numb, shed some tears. After a few minutes I comforted myself with the thought that some people did not even have sardines and baked beans to sit down to. This had always been stressed to me by my beloved grandparents. Yes, there were people out there in a lot worse situation than mine, but it was not just myself for whom I was feeling, it was also for my son.

I waited until midnight and then opened the Christmas present from Dale, which Lainey had left in the postbox on Friday, 22nd December. Lainey had made it quite clear in a note accompanying the present that Dale had chosen the contents. First, was a slim calendar, each month showing a beautiful picture of a plant; then, as I unwrapped a small box, I opened it to find a most exact small-scale figurine of a hedgehog, which I clutched in my hands and sobbed until early into the morning.

I awoke realising that, although there was no more work to bring in a wage for the rest of the week, I had to make the most of this period up to New Year and get as much rest as possible, whilst at the same time making a few plans for 1996.

I had asked my mum and two sisters not to contact me on Christmas Day, so I could try and handle my situation alone. Today I continued this by not answering the telephone. I felt anything anyone said to me would reduce me to tears. I had been so strong over the last few months, but this was such a difficult time, and I knew my family's intentions were to help. What made it more difficult was that they didn't realise that they couldn't help. I busied myself with rearranging the shed to make more space for the young that Dale's rabbit had just had.

Finding it difficult to stay alone the rest of the day, I drove down to my friends Rita and Gordon. They invited me in and we all sat and watched TV in the company of parrots, cockatiels, rabbit, and "Lady Sophie" the Persian cat. Later, Rita put on a spread and we sat down to discuss the happenings over the last few days. At midnight I bid them *'Goodnight'*, and scraped the frost off my car to drive home and retire to bed with my innermost thoughts.

(Somehow, as I write on this day, Wednesday, 27th December 1995, my inner strength seems to be helping me through sufficiently to be able at least to make plans for 1996. Thank God I am still forever hopeful.)

The telephone rang many times after I had finished work on Christmas Day, but I felt as though I had been put through a wringing machine and had not got the strength to talk to anyone. I felt mentally and physically exhausted, and also realised that I had a cold starting, which I knew I must not let mum know about, as it would cause her to worry. So, I let the telephone ring and ring, at first wondering if it might be Lainey or Dale. Then I suspected it was just my wishful thinking. If it was, and I answered, I knew I would spoil everything by getting upset and emotional; so I put up a mental barrier and did not answer the 'phone at all. I withdrew into my own world, trying to be brave and plan for myself for 1996 – the New Year now only four days away.

When beginning my college course in 1993, I felt so proud that I had made a decision that, although it was going to be financially difficult for both Lainey and myself initially, would bring its rewards after the course had finished. If only something or someone could have told me what the outcome would be, instead of hindsight two years later. Try, try and try again I was taught as a child. But how do you know even as an adult, if you're trying in the right way? Well, my Christian faith has kept me strong, and if fate has anything to do with it, whatever will be will be. This is the only way I have been able to get through life, not having a father or someone as a safety net in case I go wrong. My greatest sadness from day to day was that all I had lived for from a boy was to give my son what I had never had, and I knew I could only do that with the woman I loved. I cannot deny that I am a proud man and, at that point in time, hid from him because I was broken and knew that he couldn't take from me as when I was whole.

Before Christmas I had taken mum to Halifax for some food shopping. Whilst she saw me buying myself a rabbit for the freezer, she insisted on buying me a second one to make sure that I had plenty. I accepted by promising to take her some rabbit stew over the Christmas period, and this I did on Wednesday, 27th December but at the same time I insisted that she please leave me to my own devices for a while, as I needed time and space to myself. I tried to get her to understand that life had taken its toll on me, and I was "burned out". But mum has difficulty listening and I hoped that she had not taken "umbrage". I returned home, continued writing for a few hours and then took myself to bed.

The following day, the severe frost we had experienced over Christmas continued, with temperatures 8° below zero. Everything was frozen solid, and as I looked around the garden, taking in the frozen evergreens, I too felt to be part of its "still life". The rabbits were unable to drink, as their water bottles were frozen, and so had to take their moisture from cabbage leaves and frozen carrots I had hanging in the shed. I was able to defrost their bottles, and saw them manage to take some water before the bottles froze again.

Well, every cloud has a silver lining, and although I had only work on New Year's Eve at the hotel between then and starting my new job as gardener, I used this period to take stock of my life. As ever, my approach to 1996 will be – try, try, and try again. What appears to be the end may really be a new beginning.

Friday, 29th December 1995 at 11.00 a.m. saw me serving mulled wine at the hotel for the first wedding party, as there were two weddings booked that day: just what I needed in between Christmas and New Year. The frost was not just on the ground now, as it had been for the last week, but in the air as well, covering all the trees, telephone wires and anything else it could take its icy grip on. The front garden to the hotel was transformed into a magical "winter wonderland".

The guests of the first wedding party, which numbered only eighteen, including bride and groom, were reluctant to leave their glasses of hot mulled wine and the welcoming fire, as the photographer beckoned them all outside in turns. The bride was well and truly the centre of attraction. Not just because she was the bride but for her bravery in enduring endless photo's without her very large white mink coat, leaving her with a halter neck dress with revealing shoulders and back that left some of the guests shivering as they watched from inside. *'This is a one-off!'* insisted one elderly gent, justifying the photographer's eagerness. It truly was so lovely to see a Christmas wedding taking advantage of such a timely setting.

Well, I felt for the first time that those were to be my last days spent in full-time catering. It had been drawn on at different times to serve me for so many years, as I had depended on it for my livelihood, but times change and I was drawn to serve in another capacity, for which I now felt very ready.

After an 8.15 p.m. finish, I scraped the ice from my car to drive home and tend to Dale's rabbits before continuing writing my book until 2.30 a.m. on the Saturday morning.

Yet another time alone that brought thoughts of Lainey and Dale, and reduced me to tears under the reading lamp, leaving my eyes sore from the combination of crying and writing. Aware that I must keep strong, I eventually retired to bed to take the morrow as it came.

Later that morning I took yet another lie-in without any feeling of guilt whatsoever, which was quite out of character. Although a very heavy sleeper, once I've taken my eight hours, I like to make the most of every waking minute; but my body was not just tired, it was wrecked, and I knew that I owed it some rest if I was to expect good results from my efforts in 1996.

Could I really close the door on low pay, irregular shifts, long hours, sometimes up to six hours with no food? This was catering, and I knew my best years of working for someone else had gone. It was so easy to get into, but twenty years on saw me gasping for air, and the hope that my newfound work would breathe fresh life into me, and me into it. So it was countdown now to New Year's Day.

I knew the day itself was going to be unbelievably difficult, and had arranged to depart from the hotel once food service was over the following night, so that I could be in my own home to avoid any embarrassment of being unable to cope with my emotions.

Meanwhile, Saturday's work was casual, having only to lay tables and prepare for tomorrow. Work began at 12.00 p.m. and finished at 2.45 p.m. I spent the afternoon well wrapped, as although the frost had taken a slight thaw, the stillness was replaced with a severe and very biting strong east wind. However, I took great pleasure in watching Dale's rabbit and her four offspring venture out into the garden for a while. Soon daylight was lost and then, after a walk down to mum's, I returned home, where I continued to write until after midnight.

The next day's 1.00 p.m. start would see me working a ten-hour shift, so a good nightcap was called for.

Looking out of the bedroom window the following

morning, I was pleasantly surprised to see a covering of snow. I'd heard the east coast had had over twelve inches in the last few days. Well, whatever chaos it caused to modern day livers, I was always pleased to see it for however long it stayed. It's nature, and it signifies to me, reassuringly, that something is still in balance, when certain people in places of authority lead us to believe, rightly or wrongly, how badly damaged our climate is.

So, duty called at the hotel for what I knew was going to be my final shift there on a permanent basis. I had arranged a week ago with the manager that I could finish at 11.30 p.m., as I was afraid of being unable to keep a brave face when the midnight celebrations started.

My shift began at 1.00 p.m. with preparation. At 4.00 p.m. the manager, restaurant manager and another waiter went off duty for a couple of hours, and I was given various tasks to continue with. One of these was to light the two log fires in the restaurants at 5.00 p.m., which I did with the utmost enthusiasm, choosing and laying each log with great care. As the winter fuel smoked and crackled, it filled me with nostalgia as to how grandad, and then mum, had taught me to prepare and tend to an open fire. As these thoughts consoled me, I couldn't resist adding one more log to increase the warmth of the glow that had now built up to give a welcoming atmosphere to our New Year's Eve guests.

My attire for that and so many other evenings over the last twenty years gave me the formal appearance which was required to carry out my service, in what I can only describe as being some very comfortable and luxurious establishments. Although I always felt comfortable in my bow tie and dinner suit, I had realised quite a few years before that the purpose they had served me in earning a living full-time was now becoming more difficult due to my age. As many people do in all types of work, at some point I had recognised my good years in the industry had gone. Fortunately, unlike some, I not only had another interest in

CHRISTMAS DAY LUNCHEON

MONDAY 25TH DECEMBER 1995

LUNCHEON
FROM 12.00PM

£50.00 AND **£35.00** FOR CHILDREN UNDER 12

LOBSTER AND GRILLED POLENTA SALAD
with Balsamic and Olive Dressing

ASPARAGUS AND CHERVIL SOUP
en Croute
❄
GRATINEE OF QUEEN SCALLOPS
with an Avocado Salsa
❄
GREEN APPLE AND CALVADOS SORBET
❄
TRADITIONAL NORFOLK TURKEY
roasted with Chestnuts and Prunes

NOISETTES OF LAMB
*filled with a Herb Stuffing
and served   with a Mint
Hollandaise*
❄
PLUM PUDDING
with Brandy Custard

CARAMELISED MANDARINS
*in a Brandy Snap Basket with
Cinnamon Ice Cream*

ICED GIANDUJA SOUFFLE

A SELECTION OF ENGLISH CHEESE
with Walnut Bread
❄

NEW YEAR EVE DINNER

SUNDAY 31ST DECEMBER 1995

DINNER
FROM 7.30PM

£60.00

GALANTINE OF POUSSIN
with a Port Jelly
❄
CONSOMME BRETONNE
with Wild Mushroom Dumplings
❄
LEMON SOLE AND SEA TROUT ROULADE
on a Langostine Sauce
❄
CHAMPAGNE AND GRIOTTINE SORBET
❄
LIGHTLY SMOKED FILLET OF
ABERDEEN ANGUS
*roasted and served with a
Perigourdine Sauce*

BREAST OF GOOSE ROASTED
*on a bed of Braised Cabbage with
caramelised Apples and Sultanas*
❄
A SELECTION OF ENGLISH CHEESE
with Walnut Bread
❄
A TRIO OF SURPRISE DESSERTS
❄
COFFEE AND PETITS FOURS

DRESS BLACK TIE
*Why not make the evening more
special and stay overnight. Dinner,
accommodation and
continental breakfast £85.00*

The above is a typed version of the menu I served at the Country House Hotel, Halifax 1995 life, which I hoped could earn me a living, but had been given the opportunity and support of my wife in making the decision to change.

And so, as I turned from the blaze of the fire now warming the three dining rooms, I took an appreciative look around at the antiques with which the two daughters of the family had continued to furnish this beautiful building. The many memories of the times and different staff I had worked with there over the past fifteen years, at different intervals, came together, giving me pleasure that I had had the opportunity of getting to know this 16th century building and had felt so comfortable working in it.

At six o'clock the rest of the staff returned and a brief was given by the restaurant manager of our continuing duties up until midnight. It was now obvious to me that there was no staff meal being served, and the volume of work to be got through meant there was not even time for a quick nibble in the "Still Room". This meant I was working a ten-and-a-half hour shift with no food. Well, as they say, that's catering! Fifteen years before I would have accepted it, but this just confirmed to me that the new job offered to me on Christmas Eve was heaven-sent.

'Just do what you have to do Steve and say your goodbyes.' At 11.30 p.m. I was asked to make sure all my tables had ordered their champagne for midnight. At 11.45 p.m. I said a quiet goodbye to the restaurant manager, and left the noise of the New Year's festivities at the hotel behind.

As I climbed into my car, it was difficult not to feel a little sadness that the note on which I had left was not a happy one. The manager was not impressed by my early departure, even though I had already worked ten and a half hours, but the combination of long hours and my domestic situation had taken its toll, and I knew my last little bit of inner strength from 1995 had to go into making the decision of spending New Year alone.

The roads had a touch of black ice now after a slight thaw, and the foggy night made them very quiet as I drove steadily towards home. A few miles from home, I pulled into a lay-by and listened to Big Ben ring in the New Year on my car radio. Half of me couldn't believe what 1995 had presented me with, as my thoughts gave way to a few tears. I was finding loneliness more difficult, trying to convince myself that maybe it was because of the time of year, but I knew so deep, deep down that it was because I was not with the one I still loved. I had to bear this feeling inwardly now, as I knew I would not make any progress in the future if I could not try and be strong in my work.

I drove to mum's neighbours, a kindly couple by the name of Wilf and Margaret, whom I had befriended through mum. Their daughter was to let mum's New Year in when she arrived home. So, after this occasion and a friendly chat with Wilf and Margaret, I wished mum 'Happy New Year' and drove home. On unlocking the garden gate, the thought occurred to me that I had no one to let my New Year in. If I did it myself could it be any worse than last year? Having a mother who believes in every superstition there is, I had always pooh-poohed many of them. However, I was certainly not going to tempt fate, so in desperation I went down the garden and fumbled my way into one of my son's rabbit hutches in the dark and brought out a beautiful, huge, dark sable doe. Whispering what her mission was, I put her in first through the house door. We sat inside on the floor for a few minutes, enjoying the warmth, before I took her back to her hutch. I could never think that she could be responsible for any undesirable events that might occur in the year ahead, but could only think very fondly of her, and be glad that she happened to be there when I needed her. After all, she was one of Dale's rabbits.

Once back inside, I attempted a little writing, but soon gave way to the comforts of our bed and, as I put my head on the pillow, the thought that 1996 might have something pleasant in store.

Chapter Fourteen

(Sunday, 1ˢᵗ February, 2004. A beautiful clear blue sky, with warmth in the sun and a drive into my beloved Skipton for the week's groceries sets me up for the day; along with a short walk up the road, which, as always, is good for the soul.

Dale has not made any arrangement to see me or been in contact this weekend. I just have to give him his space, and hope he is enjoying life.

The weekend has been busy with mundane chores, but I have systematically got through them, leaving time for continuing my book; I have had a successful week on it during the evenings after work. It has been very tiring, sometimes keeping me up until midnight, but this time alone is allowing me to catch up, and hopefully to see its conclusion this year.

I do hope by reading on that you will begin to gather strength, and at least make a little light of any of your own saddened times.)

1996 was surely my turning point; although it is as well I did not know the difficulties that lay ahead over the next four years.

Monday, 8ᵗʰ January 1996, my first day at "Kingston" not only provided me with a secure start to horticulture but, as I was later to discover, began to open doors which had been closed for such a long time. It was also the place where I began to regain my sense of humour deeply ingrained in me by my grandfather but suppressed over the past few years. This was to be encouraged by the staff I worked alongside.

The five full-time members of staff at "Kingston" consisted of: Adrian; Bill, the chauffeur; the lady cleaner, who lived in the lodge house; the housekeeper; and myself. There were also Jack, the part-time gardener; and Brian, the painter and decorator, who had worked on a regular annual basis for over forty years, and now had an apprentice, Clinton.

Shortly after I started, Jack came and informed me that I had to address Mrs ? as "Madam" at all times, and that Jack and I had to be called by our surnames. From that point on Jack was "Illand", and I was "Lockwood". We were not allowed to call the ladies by their Christian names. This was because Madam had been brought up with the view that gardeners (outside workers) were lesser mortals than staff connected with the house. My first thought was that they were possibly having a joke because I was a new member of staff, but I was soon to realise I had to take this on board seriously if I valued my job and, of course, I did.

Madam, who had been widowed for the past ten years or so, was in her mid-eighties. This was someone who had not embraced change, but clearly had stood still in a time warp. As I carried out my duties in the weeks and months ahead, it became clear how archaic her running of the place was. I did, however, become very fond of her, and I think she of me, eventually inviting me into the house for a chat. She was apparently heiress to wealth, not only from her own family, but from that of her late husband, who was descended from one of the founder members of The Halifax Building Society.

There were qualities I admired about her greatly: her discipline, routine, and certain morals and principles, recognisable by her actions rather than her preaching, which I somehow felt had come to her in later years. But I also felt what a lonely figure she had become through her steadfastness, which had overshadowed much of her life in the present-day. She was, in every sense of the word, a true stalwart.

At first her stoic approach to life would upset me, until

gradually I detected through her actions and conversation that she too did have feelings, but I suspect her upbringing made it difficult for her to show them. I began to draw parallels in our present situation. She had locked herself away in her own world. I was doing exactly the same. It was almost as though this was a lesson to me.

I was unable to afford much in the way of packed lunches; sardine sandwiches would be a highlight of the week, with most days allowing only jam, a banana or even just bread and margarine. Yes, my parallel with Madam was discipline and I had to enforce it on myself uncompromisingly. I had a job with a regular wage, and had to rid myself of my college loan and bring myself up-to-date with the running of the house.

As the other staff would leave the premises at lunch time for an hour, I would eat my sandwiches in the potting shed, then I sat by the coal bunker in front of the stove, folded up my coat to make a cushion to lean my head on against the wall and afforded myself a catnap until the others returned. One day, as my catnap turned into a deeper slumber, I was startled when a voice called out, *'Are you alright Lockwood?'* On wakening I saw that Madam was half way through into the potting shed, and relieving me from any embarrassment, gave a half smile and enquired again, *'Are you alright?'* I knew she sensed something was wrong. She was too polite and well mannered to enquire further, but she was no fool, and so I came clean and told her that I was going through a separation with my wife. I was still very tender and found it difficult to discuss this with anyone new. I was fearful that if she found out, my job might be jeopardised, but she listened, and then in her stoic manner encouraged me to concentrate on Dale, before apologising for disturbing my sleep and leaving quietly. She continued to show concern for my situation for some time after, and often invited me to bring Dale to visit her.

She would spend many months abroad on holidays, but

always at the same places – Vienna and Capri – and always returned with a gift for each of her staff.

As the summer holidays approached, she asked me where I was going. When I explained that I was unable to have a holiday and wondered if it would be possible to work, she dismissed the idea, saying that everyone should have a holiday. That week, as she delivered my wage packet, she put a crisp new £50.00 note into my hand, suggesting that I take Dale away for a few days. I had told her of my farming friends in the Lake District. Although quite stunned, I quickly thanked her very much. I had never seen a £50.00 note before working for Madam, but each week she would include one in my wage packet, which always caused a reaction when trying to use it in my weekly budget. But this one was special. For minutes after she left the potting shed I sat looking at it and feeling it. This was not for the bills, this was for Dale; I could take him away. My eyes blurred as I fought back the tears. This was progress; we were having a holiday.

I duly 'phoned my friends, John and Margaret, at the farm where I had worked just outside Penrith. They invited us for a week with no charge for accommodation, allowing Dale to take a friend along too. This meant that I could treat the lads with the £50.00. Dale was still only nine years old and so never knew how I was able to give him that first holiday with his friend Matthew.

Madam loved fresh flowers in the house, and so, on Fridays, I would cut them from the garden for her, to last over the weekend. Then she began bringing huge bunches back from shopping, so there were flowers in abundance. This led to my making three to four arrangements every Friday evening after work, for which she paid me overtime.

Madam certainly had stamina, but also eccentricity running hand in hand with it. All the staff's chores had to be carried out in Dickensian style. What I witnessed has certainly provided me with sufficient material for another

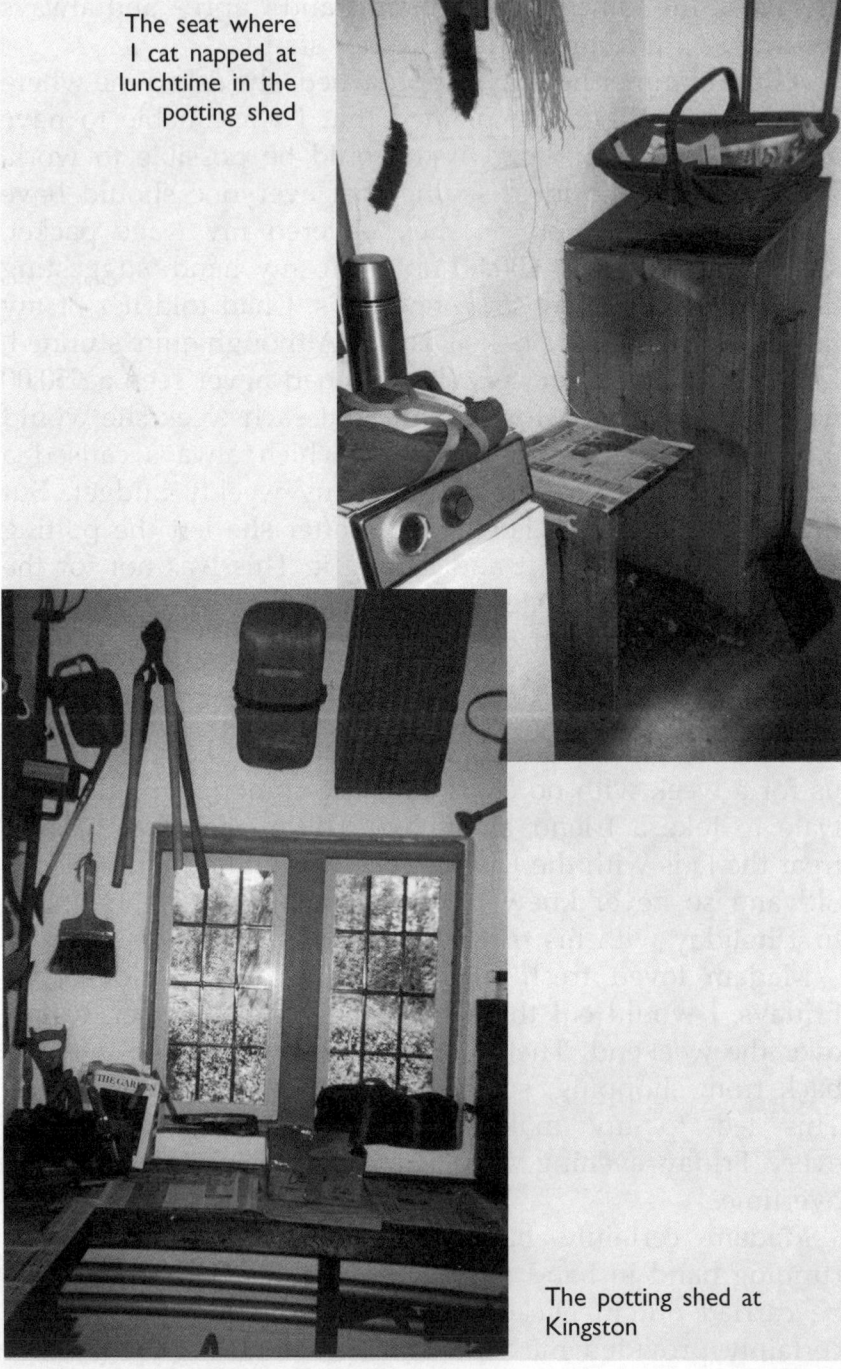

The seat where I cat napped at lunchtime in the potting shed

The potting shed at Kingston

The potting shed at
Kingston

book, so I will move on.

So bizarre were the happenings that I could not bring myself to tell anyone about them or where I worked, except my friends Rita and Gordon and mum, who I think all found it very difficult to believe. At the time I felt I was living in a dream world. With my own life out of control and the happenings at "Kingston" I was just drifting along.

Each member of staff was aware of my domestic circumstances and would provide words of comfort and encouragement, raising my spirits, throughout my time there, often creating much laughter, albeit well out of earshot of Madam. Laughing was strictly out of bounds.

"It's easy to be happy when life rolls along like a song,
But a man's only worthwhile if he can smile when
everything's going wrong."

Adrian had done small jobs for Madam as a schoolboy, after which he went on to work full-time for her. His intellect, I felt, was wasted, and although duty bound to observe her standards, it was obvious that during her latter years he had cut many corners. He was now thirty-four and unfortunately found himself unable to move on, taking the view that there could be possible financial gains from the establishment if anything happened to Madam.

It was now into April and Lainey and Dale had not been in contact.

One of my chores at "Kingston" was to provide kindling for Madam's two open fires. This was prepared in a huge old stable block set in a coach yard a few hundred yards away. There was no electricity allowed, and so I would stand in the doorway for daylight, chopping wood for hours, which I had previously sawn up from old timber. Inside was pitch black and dank, with evidence of rats. Here my thoughts were painful. Wondering about Dale and how I was going to find my next stepping-stone.

Apart from Lainey allowing Dale to visit me for an hour

one evening in January, they were not in contact again until 12th April, when Lainey 'phoned and let Dale speak to me. Dale asked if he could visit me on 21st April, which was the day before his birthday. Of course, I was delighted, even though it was only for the day. It was heaven to be with him and we had a wonderful time, but the anguish after his leaving was unbearable – the closing of the door and my cries, leaving me mentally and physically drained, and wondering if and how I would ever cope with this situation.

I knew that for Dale to see me upset was not good for him, so my next thoughts were to work at being strong for Dale as well as myself in the hope that, if he saw me happy, he would want to spend more time with me. I now had to begin to think very positively if I was going to see my son grow up. This I did through prayer and encouragement from a few friends and mum. At first it was like a tug-of-war going on in me, but then, gradually, and only gradually, by keeping busy and thinking positively did I begin to feel stronger.

Throughout the rest of 1996 I designed and implemented eight small gardens. Eventually, Dale began spending more time with me, staying over at weekends and bringing his friends. Lainey and I had taken Dale to swimming lessons from an early age, which he was still continuing and doing very well at. But now his grandparents from London had become more involved with Dale's activities, booking him into tennis lessons and generally spending more time with him, which left me feeling inadequate. However, the times we had together became happier. There was definitely a buzz now when we were arranging to see each other, and however little or much we decided to do, it was our time together that was so precious.

It was at this stage that I recognised what effect these circumstances were having on Dale. As we would have a game of football in the park or watch a film, there would be, on occasions with me, moments of relapse, which Dale would immediately detect, and would follow up with the words, *'Come on Dad'*, or give me an affectionate cuddle. It was these moments that would tug at my heart- strings, making me realise how much Dale was trying for me, and how difficult it could be for him. He was showing concern for me which, in turn, helped me to try and conceal my emotions, as I did not want Dale burdened at this tender age. We had begun to form a special bond; something had come alive in me since I regained full-time work.

Dale, school photograph
Hebden Royd Junior
School 1996

Only now, reading back through my diaries, has it become very obvious to me how much pressure Dale too must have been under by having to remain silent with me over matters and happenings his mother, her parents and her new husband were forcing on him whilst they were choosing another direction in life.

I was now able to repair the car well enough to run for a while longer. Outside my working hours I became full-time washer-up; cook; house cleaner; chauffeur and entertainer; and although I was exhausted, I loved and cherished every moment with my son, whether he decided to bring friends or come alone, it was the time he gave me which allowed me to watch him grow that meant so much to me.

To allow our relationship to become stronger and happier, I was only too aware of how I must also continue to grow outside the time I was spending with Dale. I was desperate to find my next stepping-stone, and relentless in pursuit of my aim to one day design a large garden. If I was to achieve this, then I would have to balance my time with

Dale gets to grips with his sledge in the fields behind our cottage, along with some other locals. The snow lasting for a week Wed 1st Jan 1997.

Dale in the garden at our cottage. Winter 1996 November.

Dale whilst furthering my career.

I was extremely careful as to how much contact Dale had with my family at this point, as mum's relationship with us all was often turbulent, and I did not want Dale exposed to any further distress. However, he often wanted to see his Nanna Laura, and my two sisters and his cousins, who gave him contact with my family, allowing him to form his own views.

The remainder of 1996 left me with happy memories of days taking Dale cycling, swimming, playing tennis, snowballing and sledging, visiting the cinema, going for walks, and just cramming as many things into our time together as we could.

Dale's mum and I had always had pet names for each other. Throughout our marriage, she would call me "Bright Eyes" and I would call her "Lainey". At some point in early 1997, through written correspondence, she referred to herself as "Helen". I took this as the first sign of her wanting to sever contact with me. On Wednesday, 19th March 1997, at 7.00 p.m. she visited me and asked for a divorce, along with her payment for half of the house, plus a list of things she wanted to take. It was as though I was talking to a stranger. I agreed, and after she had left, determined not to let a sickening feeling get the better of me, I drove myself down the valley to my friends Rita and Gordon, who were, as ever, very supportive.

1997 was to prove a difficult year in terms of overcoming many obstacles. The evening following that I spent with Helen discussing divorce proceedings whilst I watched Dale having his swimming lesson at Halifax Baths, and when I returned home found that I had been burgled. The house was a mess but, as it happened, I must have disturbed them on my return and so very little was missing.

It was now nearly two years since Helen had left, and so the divorce could now take place legally with the consent of both of us, unless I decided to put a stop on it for five years, which apparently the legal system allowed. This, to me, would have just prolonged the agony, and as I recalled a doctor in my practice sympathising with my situation once in conversation saying, *'Steve, if you love someone, set them free, and then whatever will be will be'*, I took her advice.

Shortly after, I began to receive threatening letters from Helen's solicitors, demanding that I move out of the house so that she could receive her payment. I found it extremely difficult in my naivety to believe that she could act towards me like this. She obviously had the backing of her parents, both morally and financially. I was totally alone and had to make the decision to get a solicitor to act on my behalf. This was so foreign to me and initially baulked me into silence when legal advisors spoke against her in very harsh terms. It was so difficult trying to suppress my feelings for her, which she had probably lost long ago for me.

I had continued applying for posts throughout my time at Madam's as, due to her age, I felt I would be forced into difficult circumstances should I stay until her latter years. I was now concerned that, to achieve my goal, I might have to move away, as the position I was looking for was most likely to be found much further south or north. The last thing I wanted now was to put distance between Dale and myself. My ideal was to carry out this type of work somewhere in the Yorkshire Dales, which would make travelling to Dale easy, but there were few positions in this area. I had begun taking the local paper for The Dales, as well as national journals, and one week I followed up an advert for a full-time gardener, which was between Keighley and Skipton

One lunchtime, in exchange for my usual sleep in the potting shed, I walked to a telephone box just outside the grounds of "Kingston". On making my call, I was answered by a lady with a delightful telephone manner. After initial enquiries from both parties, an interview was arranged for 6.30 p.m. on Tuesday, 29th April 1997.

By now I was receiving regular letters from Helen's solicitors, which were very distressing. Because of my lack of funds, my solicitor was trying to support me through

Legal Aid, but this proved unsuccessful. I was desperate for professional help. Somehow I had to get through this, but it was so difficult trying to raise my spirits alone, and not let Dale see me affected.

Although I was looking forward to my interview, I was questioning whether my confidence would see me through, due to the huge turmoil I was experiencing. Still, it was just another gardener's position, and so I was not building up too much hope as I knew my next move must be a challenge.

It was a beautiful, clear, sunny day as I left for the interview, and a comfortable feeling came over me. I had travelled this road many times over the last thirty-three years. My directions were off the main road approaching Skipton. Approximately two hundred yards up this lane I found an old manor. I drew up in front of the house. The only shoes I had to my name were a pair of heavy brogues, which had been a part of me since I bought them whilst working on the nursery some seven years before, but I had cleaned them well, and hoped they would pass as serviceable a while longer. They didn't seem out of place, as I stood marvelling in front of the house for a few seconds before I was greeted with a firm handshake by a gentleman who had appeared from a side entrance. He had a fresh complexion and an eager look. Once inside, I met his wife, a warm and welcoming lady, and although they introduced themselves by their Christian names, I felt it only befitting for me to address them by their surnames.

I was completely seduced by the manor garden, and its potential. As they gave me a guided tour, I was champing at the bit, devouring everything before me as my eyes scanned endless possibilities.

Heavily involved in the family business, the gentleman had little time for the garden, whilst the lady was equally busy with the running of the house. Residents for some thirty years, they had seen the garden pass through several hands over more recent years, and it was now in need of major attention. There were many areas which were badly neglected, though, fortunately, this had not dampened the owners' spirits for getting it back on track. I could see how desperate they were for work to go ahead, but would they be willing to let me take it on?

The interview was thorough. I did not consciously attempt to convince them that I was the man for the job, only could not restrain my enthusiasm on such a topic, but knew that this was in the lap of the gods. It was obvious to me that the gentleman was a man who could roll his sleeves up, a Yorkshire man with his feet on the ground. There was a lot of eye contact; we both knew this job had to be done, but would he consider me of a similar ilk? There had been several applicants and so I was now to wait for a second interview.

After returning home, I continued at "Kingston", not mentioning anything so as to avoid an anticlimax but, shortly after, the lady at the manor contacted me for a second interview, and I accepted.

However, later that day my thoughts became torn. I knew full and only too well that I was able to do the job. What I did not know was what restrictions and difficulties lay ahead of me now with divorce proceedings and finance, etc. So much was in the balance now if I were lucky enough to be accepted for this job. The strain of my domestic problems could jeopardise my job prospects. There was no option, I had to 'phone back to the manor and cancel my second interview, whilst being honest with them about my domestic situation, which I had not mentioned fully on my previous visit. But my cancellation was rebuffed by the lady, who suggested that I went along and talked things through with them. I accepted gratefully, and duly went along to meet them both for a second time. They were very accommodating regarding my circumstances, about which I was extremely embarrassed. They offered me contacts and support for my divorce proceedings, for which I felt greatly humbled.

Whichever way I looked at life, I had reached a major crossroads and I had to draw on some true "Yorkshire grit". All my life I had strived to find peace and stability away from the unconventional upbringing I had witnessed as a child. Now, here I was being put in the ring for a fight chosen by someone with whom I had been dearly in love, and who was the mother of my son. At this crucial time I was desperate for something on which to focus. There it was, staring me in the face. The manor garden, I am convinced, was Heaven sent. It was up to me to prove to the owners that I was up to it. So, I threw down the gauntlet and the challenge was on, as we shook hands and agreed that I would take up my position at the manor on 19th May, 1997.

(Sunday, 22nd February, 2004, 11.00 p.m. It is mum's 75th birthday tomorrow, and her last minute attempt to try and bring all the family together today for a meal [except my brother Larry and his wife, who were in Somerset] has gone disastrously wrong.

My younger sister, Sandra, attempted to bring along, against mum's wishes, the daughter of her current partner. This has caused friction, and ultimately left mum unwilling to go out anywhere. I have returned home sadly and feeling very tired from the outcome. Nevertheless, I have still managed to write some more of my book before retiring to bed.)

Returning to "Kingston", I broke the news to Madam. She was both angry and upset. This was very traumatic for us both, as she begged and pleaded for me to stay, to the extent that she contacted her son to come up from Warwickshire. Together they offered me a house and to pay the full costs of my divorce proceedings. This was pure buying power in an attempt to take control of someone's life without consideration for their making progress. As I declined the offer, a rage came over her, and as she turned away dismissively, had it not been for her senior years, I feel sure that she would have stamped her feet on the spot

Myself at the potting shed door at Kingston, with the laundry next door.

My work at Kingston included cleaning grates out around the grounds and filling the coal bunker.

and thrown a tantrum.

Poor Adrian. He was somewhat dejected when he heard that I was leaving. He was mostly responsible for my being able to face the day's work, creating humour in conversation, helping me with some of the unusual tasks in our daily routine, as I would in turn with him, and encouraging me to keep strong for Dale on days when he knew I was very low. Many of the house staff did not care for him due to some of his wrongdoing towards Madam and his own lack of tidiness, but I felt pity for the pathetic situation into which she had put him as a schoolboy. Now unable to escape her clutches, and hanging on to the fantasy of financial gain, Adrian was just not strong enough to move on with his life. He had confided in me his love of gardening, but did not have the confidence to take it up. Madam was aware of this and would allow him to help the gardener prune the

A chore included with my gardening was to fill a hand cart with fuel from an old stable block some 400yds away and push it back to the house to fill the coal bunker for Madam's fires. The stable block was also used for storing fire-wood which I had to keep chopped frequently. There was no electricity or heating allowed here.
1996-1997

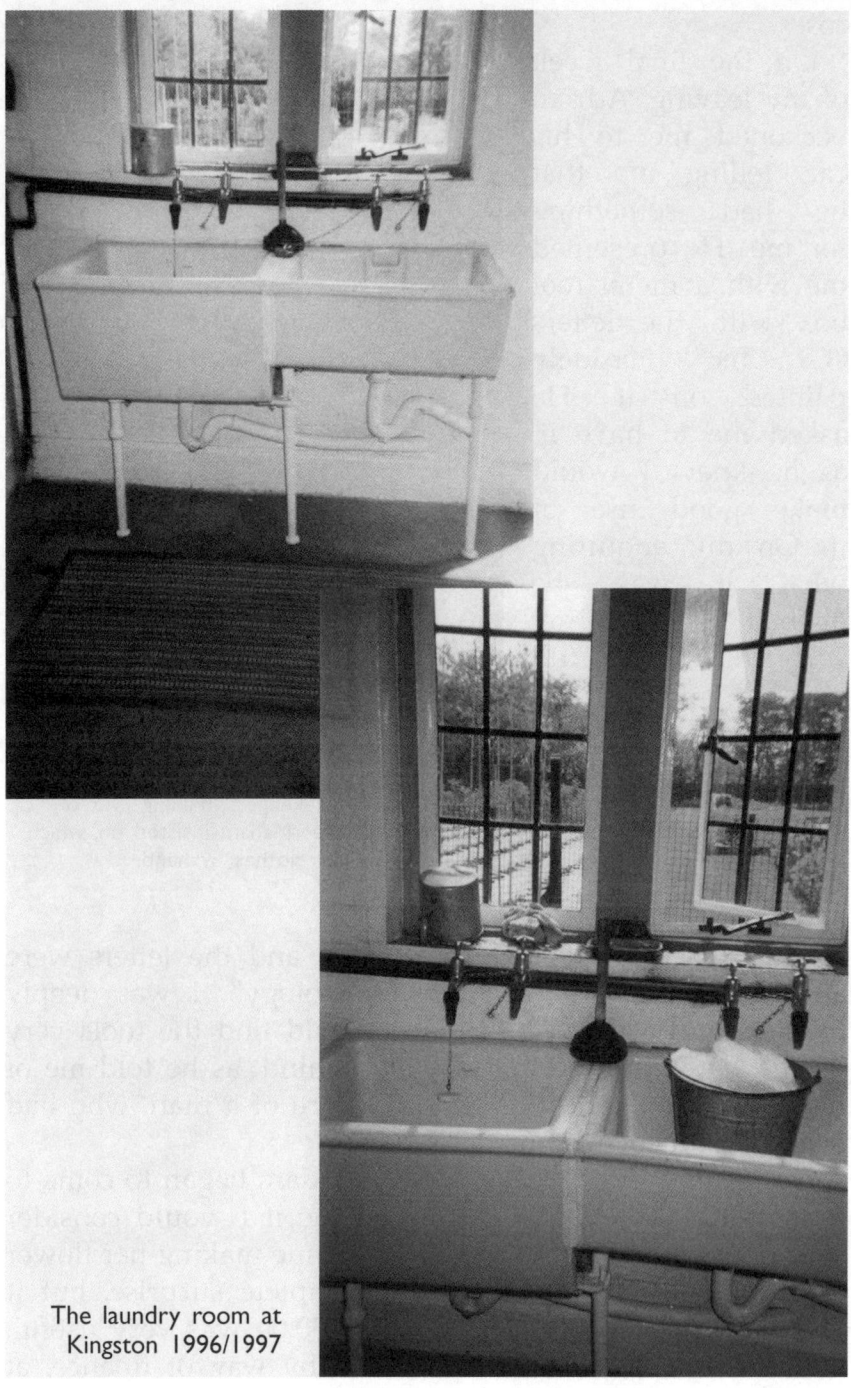

The laundry room at
Kingston 1996/1997

roses.

On the final week of my leaving, Adrian beckoned me to his car, telling me that he had something for me. He presented me with a metal tool box with the letters "G Tec" crudely painted on it. He asked me to have it, as he knew I would make good use of it. On my enquiring what it was, he opened it. To my surprise, it was full of garden tools and knick-knacks he had collected, all relating to gardening. He had never told anyone, but said that it was a dream of his to

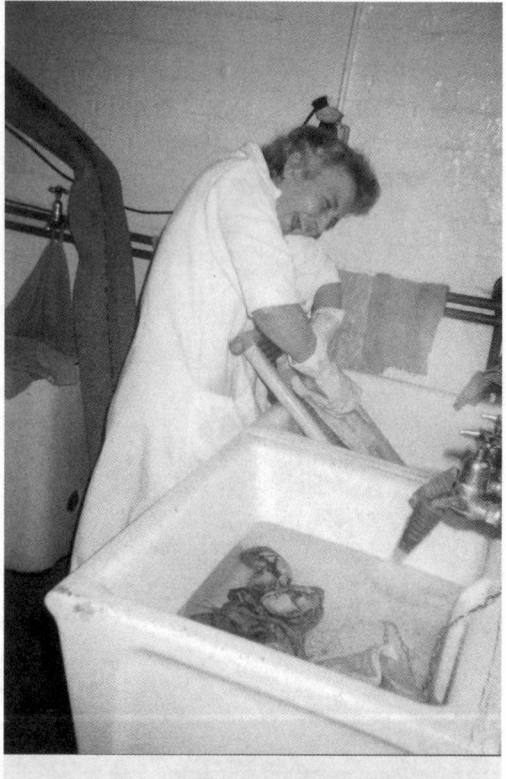

One of the housekeepers, making light of one of the chores Madam insisted on, which was to wash her clothes by hand.

set up as a self-employed gardener, and the letters were an abbreviation for "Garden Technology". I was deeply touched and assured him that I would find the tools very useful. It was sad seeing him left behind, as he told me of his envy of my future; a forlorn figure of a man, who had been consumed by someone's power.

During my three weeks' notice, Madam began to come to terms with my leaving and asked me if I would consider returning on Friday evenings to continue making her flower arrangements. This took me by complete surprise, but it was the least I could do, and the £30.00 was very useful. However much power Madam had by way of finance, at the end of the day this was a frightened person clinging on to a familiar face in her latter years. So I agreed to her request and travelled from the manor every Friday evening after work for the next four and a half years. Madam passed away at "Kingston" at 3.00 p.m. on Thursday, 4th October, 2001.

Chapter Fifteen

(I do hope that my pauses for thought as follows, at certain times in my writing, do not prove irritating. They are a spontaneous reaction to my present environment, and I hope that by including them in my book, they will prove valuable to any readers who may be experiencing a difficult period in their lives. It is these times of thought that help to heal.

Friday, 27th February, 2004. There has been an overnight fall of snow. Only an inch, but it is the dry, clean type, which has been rare these last few years, supposedly due to the scientists' evidence of global warming. For me it is more than welcome. The weather conditions over the last week, with a combination of frost and a cold northwesterly wind, have left the ground rock hard.

After a bowl of porridge, I enjoyed my walk to work. Once up at the manor, I found the snow was new and unspoilt. I made my way into the clearing in the woods where I had left a fire burning the night before. The dying embers were just enough for me to revive it with wood left around its heart. Once it came to life I put on the remainder of the logs.

The dense woodland blocked out the sun from the manor house between November and January when the sun was at its lowest, but now it was gaining height, and by 10.30 a.m., as it sparkled through the bare branches, I faced upwardly towards it, returning the sparkle as I smiled to myself and prayed that Dale might take delight in such simple pleasures; they are truly the richest.

The flames from the fire now gave me warmth as I tidied up the remainder of the wood. It was peaceful, with no one to interrupt my thoughts. I left the fire and continued with my day's work.

Later that morning I returned to the potting shed, where the farm buildings behind the manor offered me a view between them. As it took my eye above the hub of the busy valley below and out towards Skipton, there, under the intense clear blue sky and the winter sun, stood the Dales fells, where I had spent so many years from my youth onwards. Among them was "Sharphaw", where I ran my first fell race at the age of seventeen.)

1997 and 1998 saw a big improvement in the way that both Dale and I were handling our relationship. For my part, I had to exercise great patience and understanding of Dale's situation, very steadily building towards our future. My employers were to play a huge role in helping me through this. It was also a time of extreme pressure from different directions. The letters from Helen's solicitors were now frequent, and very aggressive.

Travelling the twenty-two miles to and from work was very tiring. There was also an added trauma, which had been in the background for many years back at the cottage. A family who lived either side of me had taken umbrage some six years before, when I asked if they would stop their Alsatian dog purposely aggravating our dog, Jack. Now, as I was living alone, they took the opportunity of revenge. This led to them blocking my access on leaving and returning home; smashing my car window; using threatening and abusive behaviour towards me both in person and on the telephone; and banging Dale's bedroom window with sticks. It later came to light that they were having problems in their family, and I can only assume that they were taking them out on me.

Unaware of all these happenings, Dale would probably at the time have found it difficult to understand why I seemed distant from him on occasions. But we battled through and experienced some memorable times.

In the midst of this crisis there was help; unknowingly I had found it the day I made the 'phone call with enquiries regarding the vacancy at the manor. The garden of some eight acres may have seemed daunting for many a gardener to take on single-handed. However, I saw it as a way of channelling my energies away from everything and everyone that was persecuting me. This was the opportunity to grow outside my time with Dale. I had not only found my next stepping-stone, but had reached the other side of that fast-running stream.

During my interviews, we had discussed the fact that several areas of the garden would undergo major renovation. This I dealt with as individual projects, running alongside the general maintenance, which in itself was long overdue. This included two fifty-metre long conifer hedges, one of which had been allowed to reach some twenty-seven feet in height, along with a badly neglected beech hedge. The garden needed lots of TLC – it also needed some sense of direction, along with character and substance, and an injection of funds.

To begin all this, it was vital for me to establish a composting system, which was at that time limited to two small bays of kitchen compost. With my employers agreement, work began, and the excitement of experiencing uncertainty when being adventurous in planting lay ahead, along with producing some damned good compost.

> *"A real gardener is not a man who cultivates flowers;*
> *He is a man who cultivates the soil ...*
> *If he came into a garden of roses he would sniff excitedly*
> *and say:*
> *'Good Lord, what humus!'"*

Dale was now ten years old, and approaching his last year at Hebden Royd Church of England Junior School in Hebden Bridge, which Helen and I had so carefully chosen for him in his infant years. It had a good reputation, the teachers and headmistress had been long serving and caring, which is an ideal start to any child's schooling, and one which we valued for Dale. However, during Dale's last year his headmistress had decided to move on and the whole infrastructure collapsed. Helen and I were at the stage of trying to enrol Dale for his secondary school, which I assumed would be the one in the valley that was an automatic intake for pupils from Dale's school. To my sheer dismay, Helen told me of her plans to change work and that she was trying to get Dale accepted at another school on the other side of Halifax. I was totally gutted. He would be leaving most of his friends behind and coping with a new environment on top of the stress of his parents divorcing. I could not believe Dale would have to cope with something so seemingly heartless.

This now presented me with the further legal fight of trying to continue Dale's schooling in the valley. I was eventually to lose.

At the beginning of October half term, Helen had taken Dale to London to her parents along with her lover. At 9.00 p.m. on a Monday evening she 'phoned to tell me she was getting married, and would bring Dale up on the train to meet me at Leeds Station on the Wednesday. I could hardly bear the time in between. As I met them at 6.25 p.m., Helen handed me Dale's suitcase and, quite unconcerned, swiftly turned away to catch her train back to London.

Dale was so pleased to see me and I him. I have never encouraged him to eat fast food but after we hugged, we had a burger in McDonald's before going straight home.

It was just one of the many times that he would not realise the hurt I was feeling for him. I felt he was being passed around like a piece of baggage. It had now become obvious to me that Helen's priority was with another man and Dale was a matter of course. Things seemed to be operating with no emotion for Dale. Of even greater concern for me

187

was that it appeared he could not be truthful with me, as became very clear as time went on.

A family we had known for many years, with two children of Dale's age, lived near my new work. Judith, Neil, Eleanor and Jonathon had kept in touch with me. We had arranged to go to Hebden Bridge bonfire on Saturday, 8th November, but Dale had been unable to tell me that he was going to be at his mum's wedding in London that day. This was just one of the many memorable times I had to put behind me. I went along with my friends but feeling very sad that Dale was unable to be there.

Helen's plans continued to unfold as on 8th December she told me that they were moving from her parents' home into a new house. I felt increasingly sad and annoyed that Dale had not told me. This was a difficult situation for a child, though I was beginning to feel that he was happy to go along with his mum's plans. However, that Christmas of 1997 saw us spend the whole season together from 25th to 28th December.

One frosty night in the October, as I had been returning from work, a six-week old black and white kitten found its way into our garden and refused to leave. Dale begged me to keep her, and after several unsuccessful attempts at finding her owners, she took up residence with us. Due to her facial markings, we named her "Smudge". I had never had a cat before, so this was a new experience. What a lovely time she and Dale had over that Christmas. It was heaven to be with Dale, but there was an underlying feeling that it was a convenient arrangement for his mum to allow her and her new husband to be alone.

Between the traumas of that year I had made it as eventful as possible for Dale. It was not always accepted with great enthusiasm, but once involved, he enjoyed the times. These included: getting him through his cycling test, visiting the Edinburgh Tattoo, holidaying in The Lakes, and weekend activities together. We were definitely making progress and it was a lovely feeling.

Dale and myself with pet rabbit Bramble in the garden at our cottage. 1997.

1998 saw the pressure mounting on having to move out of the house. Helen had said that I would not have to, but it was the only way I could raise the money she was asking for. Besides, it would help me to move forward with my life, if I could only keep strong enough to embrace this dramatic change and upheaval. I knew I had tried every which way to save our marriage, which had been rejected at every point along the way. In many ways, it was such a relief now to put the remaining legalities in the hands of a professional, and so I began operating under the advice of my employers contact.

My time now was dedicated to Dale and gardening and sometimes I worked until 10.00 p.m. in the evenings before leaving to drive home, and then rose at 5.00 a.m. the following morning to prepare myself before returning to the manor. Dale was beginning to stay for whole weekends sometimes now and feeling much more relaxed. We began

Dale with his pet rabbit Bramble in the garden, in his bedroom, and in the livingroom with one of his friends Alistair at our cottage 1997/1998

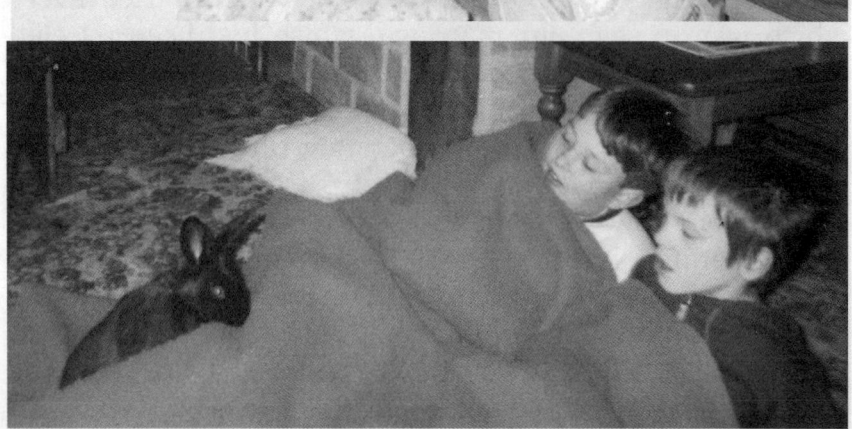

Rita and Gordon share Christmas with us. our cottage 1997.

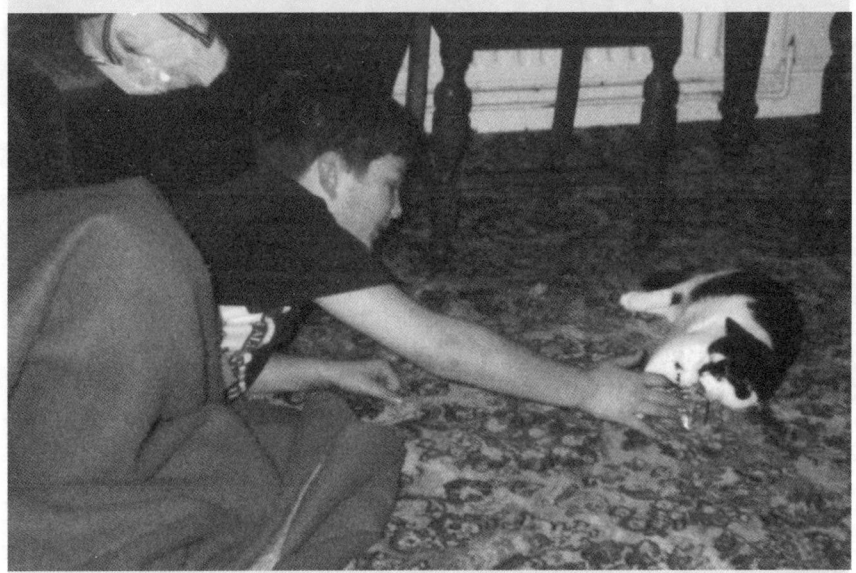

Dale with his favourite blue blanket which he shared with all his friends. 1997 playing with his cat Smudge.

playing squash and made the most of the outdoors. Dale was no less than brilliant and willing to become involved in most things I suggested – one being the Three Peaks, which he admirably completed with me one Saturday in June.

In the September, Dale began his new secondary school, which he seemed to accept in his stride. He quickly made some new friends and proudly introduced them to me. One became a regular visitor, which was good for Dale, as I felt he needed some company of his own age now whilst spending his time with me. This eventually led to his friend, David, coming away on holidays with us.

Mum's relationship with us all remained turbulent, which I found difficult and saddening whilst dealing with my responsibilities at the time. But, looking back, mum must also have found life difficult at that time. Yes, my life was upside down, and I suppose I was engrossed in sorting out my own problems, so much so that I failed to see why some days when I visited mum, the door would be locked and all the curtains drawn.

I did think the world of my son, and was trying not to let him see my low times, but I only had Dale to consider. At times mum must have felt the load five fold, as she looked on and worried over all of us, trying to help us in our individual circumstances, even though we were all now adults. She too must have been feeling the strain that year, as one of my sisters and her husband were in great financial difficulties with a hotel business; my other sister was in between marriages; one brother was preparing to leave for Australia after the collapse of a relationship; and I was also preparing to move away after a broken marriage. Yes, I can now understand why she sometimes felt that she wanted to block the world out when she was alone.

(It is Sunday, 4th April, 2004 and I have managed to pick up my pen once again. A hard spell at work a few weeks ago left me a little low after completing one of my projects. I was devastated at having to take to my bed with a viral infection for a whole week. Thankfully, mum was able to come and stay with me – dividing her time between us once again as only a mother knows how. So my writing was carefully put away under lock and key until today, when I am once again able to press on ever nearer to my conclusion.)

Since Helen and I had moved into our own home from the Golf Club, mum had moved house twice in the same valley. These frequent house moves always brought extra responsibilities for us all, knowing mum needed help with fixtures and fittings, gardening and moral support, but we all rallied and did our bit in the hope that she would have found a place to settle.

In one of mum's usual efforts to try to gather her brood around her, she arranged a farewell meal for my brother, Darren, who was due to fly out to Australia to begin a new life. She booked this meal in the local pub, next door to where she was now living in the Calder Valley, for the 24th September, 1998. We were all there except for Larry and his wife, who found it too far to travel from Somerset. Mum was very, very brave on the day, but she did not need to tell me how many tears she shed after Darren had gone, thinking that this could be the last time that she would see him. The following week he left.

In early November I began my appointments with my employers contact regarding house finances. These had to be fitted in with solicitors' appointments regarding our divorce. As anyone who has been through this procedure will realise, it is such a degrading thing to go through with, as your personal life is brought under the spotlight by strangers. I just hoped and prayed that I could be strong enough for the people who were helping me; I had to trust them.

At this stage Dale had suddenly stopped contacting me for a month or more. It later seemed it was due to misunderstandings in communication on either side. These times left me very sad and anxious but, as time went by, I realised it was a pattern that Dale would repeatedly make. Although I found this inconsistency very difficult, I was prepared to tolerate it rather than insist on access to him every weekend through a Court order. Many fathers may take the view that it is their right to fight to see their child on a weekly basis. My feeling was that this can put the child under more pressure. Fortunately, Helen never tried to stop Dale having contact with me, so he was allowed to come and go as he wished, which I felt was more in the child's interest. Once again, with patience and effort, we were back on course.

Christmas Eve saw Dale arrive at 7.00 p.m. We had a lovely evening together preparing the turkey and trifle, putting presents round the Christmas tree and drinking homemade snowballs, which Dale liked me to make with extra advocaat. On Christmas Day, all excited, Dale woke me to the smell of turkey, and anxious to open his presents. Mum and Sandra joined us later in the morning. Then, as Dale's mum collected him at 2.00 p.m., I made preparations to have Rita and Gordon and mum for lunch, which proved a pleasant end to the day.

Boxing Day was spent at my employers for tea, before travelling up to "Penfold Cottage" in The Lakes to spend a few days with my friends Tony and Mary.

February 1999 saw my sister Sandra and me arranging a party for mum's 70th birthday, unbeknown to her. On the evening before, Dale and I chatted excitedly into the night discussing Nanna Laura's 70th birthday party to which I was taking him. It was a total surprise to mum, and a lovely party with friends and family at her local pub next door.

In March, my car of the last seven years broke down beyond repair. I accepted the £200.00 offered by the scrap yard, and took to the train and bus to get myself to work. This involved a walk across Bradford to catch a connection. There were days when I would arrive at work soaked with rain. This lasted for a couple of months but I would have continued until I collapsed in order to save my job had

A family photograph.

Mum's 70th Birthday party. Aunty Rita left, Mum on right.

a very basic van not come my way, for which I was extremely grateful. This allowed me to see Dale more often, and we were to spend many holidays and weekends in The Lakes and Dales, taking his friend David. The van would be packed excitedly with the addition of two blue blankets, from which Dale had found comfort ever since he was a baby, and a couple of pillows so that they could lie down on the journey, as they laughed and joked whilst I drove them northwards.

Mum on left and Rita and Gordon dance the night away. Mum's 70th birthday, Brierly.

One such holiday they spent sailing on Ullswater in a dinghy, which I bought them from Tony's shop. As I lay on the shore, picnic prepared, the day seemed idyllic for them, but for me as a parent, I was constantly looking out for signs of danger, knowing that they were my sole responsibility, and ready to leap to their rescue at a moment's notice. I was so relieved when they were back on dry land. However, I could not let Dale think that I was incapable of letting him take part in life's adventures. They were testing times, as most parents will know, and standing on the sidelines can be very painful. Also, there were still difficult times, but we were overcoming them much better now.

The support from mum, my employers, Rita and Gordon, and Tony and Mary was invaluable, as they helped me to see things from Dale's point of view – a child torn between

Our last spring time at our cottage. Dale left with his friend Dave March 1999.

his parents' love and with so much on offer from his mum and her parents. I knew that I just had to cope somehow for Dale's sake.

The financial agreement between Dale's mum and me was completed and returned to the Court. This enabled me, to some extent, to begin my search for another house closer to my work at the manor, and also to put our cottage up for sale so that I could pay Dale's mum her money from the sale of the property. However, it proved to be a long and anxious time, which I tried to bear without Dale being aware of it. He was so good, helping me choose a house and discussing the excitement of a new house through a child's eyes. I knew that I had to try and bury the memories and move on, but I felt so alone and prayed every day for strength. God bless Dale.

Early November 1999, and the week's work had been going well. I felt I was catching up with some jobs that had been dragging on from the summer. A weekend away at "Penfold Cottage" had refreshed me and I was now looking forward to beginning some more winter projects at the manor.

The past two years had been fraught with unpleasant letters from Helen's solicitors. It had been a wearing time, and, my employers and friends, along with their advisor, had supported me tirelessly. Without this support I'm sure that I would not have recovered from the torment of my ordeal as quickly, if at all, or been as strong. Now, the reality of what I had known was to come over the last four and a half years – the home, our first, which we renovated together and where our son spent the first eight years of his life, had now to be sold.

Since the clocks had gone back, my winter finishing time had begun, which was 4.30 p.m. I never really minded the dark winter nights, but after Dale and his mum had left it was very lonely and was something I had to get used to. Helen's money had to be paid by December 2000, next year. So, the house went up for sale immediately in September. The first day, a couple came to look and applied to buy it, so moving seemed imminent.

It was very painful, handling all this alone, and trying to stay cheerful to the outside world. The saddest thing was that what used to be a loving family home now became a house that just haunted me with memories, and so the day I was to move out could not come soon enough. At that stage, although I had shown interest in a house close to work, I was not sure whether finances would meet the demand.

Whilst travelling around house hunting, I could not resist calling in on the occasional nursery to purchase plants for work. This brought me into contact with like-minded people, two of whom, Steve and Kim, I visited often and we became friends. Steve and Kim had begun their own nursery at the same time as I started work at the manor, and became part of my small circle of friends as I began to rebuild my life.

Dale was once again going through one of his phases of not contacting me, so joining Rita and Gordon for tea at our usual haunt in the Cragg Valley on my way home on Bonfire Night was something to look forward to. Passing through Hebden Bridge I could see the huge "Round Table" bonfire across the canal to the playing fields. The police were all in readiness with floodlights and "no parking" cones stretched out along the main road. The atmosphere was building and excitement beginning to show on people's faces. This was the familiar scene we had shared as a family for many years. It was a perfect night for bonfires, every child's delight. It had been an almost perfect day, and would have been if I was with my son, but Dale was now twelve years old, and despite our domestic circumstances, I had begun to realise that he, like every child of his age, was beginning to spend more time with his friends as he grew. Something I found difficult to prepare for.

After our pub food in front of the open fire, I left Rita and Gordon to drive home. Dale's cat, Smudge was waiting as I unlocked the door. I was eager to let her in as she hated the fireworks. Once inside, she took delight in jumping in and out of the cardboard boxes I had ready for packing. However painful it was going to be, it had to be done. I was glad that it had become a priority because two of my friends had invited me to go along to bonfires. It was so kind, but I knew in my heart that the pain of being at either bonfire without Dale would have been harder to bear than that of packing, which I looked at as going forward. I only hoped with all my heart that Dale would join me at some stage in moving house and let me involve him in it as his project as well as mine, hopefully making it exciting for us both.

During the last week I had received a telephone call from my estate agents to say that my buyers had been to their solicitors and paid the first part of their deposit for the house. For the first time it suddenly hit me that I was actually moving; it had finally come. Four and a half years of uncertainty, legal battles and emotional pain had taken its toll, but I thanked God every day that I was able to work throughout it all.

After giving my employers the news of the 'phone call, they seemed a little bewildered as to why I wasn't showing great excitement, but a broad smile of relief was enough for me at this stage. I had so many mixed feelings to cope with, and suddenly they all seemed to surface. Most of all I wanted Dale to know of the progress in moving house. Then there was the ordeal of storing all my things until I could be sure that I was moving into the house I had in mind, and then to continue packing, which was becoming harder. I had arranged for mum to come up on Sunday to help me. She was so willing and looking forward to it in the sense of having some company.

Sunday was the usual grey, damp sort of day we had been having recently, but I knew I had to collect mum at 11.30 a.m. for packing. However, I was unaware of what was due to happen. As I arrived I was told that she had received a somewhat surprising telephone call. My first thoughts were of Dale, but then mum could hardly contain herself as she told me that my eldest brother from Somerset was staying in Halifax for the weekend and was coming to see her for an hour before having to rush back. So the packing plans were delayed as my brother Larry and his wife with their daughter and her husband, took us into the next-door pub for a drink. This was a day I had been hoping would happen for many years, and knew mum felt the same, as a family feud had caused them to not speak for the last twelve years. My reservations were that the reunion had to be held over a round of drinks in a pub whose atmosphere they both enjoyed, but which had inevitably caused trouble many times in the past. They will never learn by their mistakes, but who was I to judge, just because I am a non-drinker? So, I sat it out whilst the glasses of beer were passed around. I had felt so much pain from my family in the past that, looking at their faces, beaming with glee because they were with their loved ones, had, unbeknown to them at that moment, made me feel so very cold and empty. All my love was locked up. It had been since Helen had left, except for sharing Dale on Sundays, and even that had gone now. I was deep in thought and totally outside their conversation, but I managed to regain my composure to save any humiliation, which I knew Larry, my eldest brother, was capable of causing, but had refrained from on this delicate meeting.

Mum and Larry embraced each other as they began to leave. That spontaneous reaction of love between two people is for me always a pleasure to see, but in this case, was also somewhat hurtful, as I know that for all the love that I have for mum, she never makes that gesture to me. There is a bond between them, but I am still grateful for the help mum gives and other ways in which she shows her love for me. I hoped that they would now keep contact, although I did feel that a not-too-regular basis would work better. It couldn't have happened at a better time for me as I knew mum was finding it very difficult that I was moving away. So things "have to be" as they say.

I took mum up home and could tell that she was excited about the meeting as we continued to pack. She was, as ever, helpful in such circumstances and I cooked us a meal in between boxes. After discussing the day's events and twelve boxes later, I took her home and then was more than ready to retire.

The rooms were all now very bare and made the cottage feel cold, even though we had been working with no heating on. I had missed Dale so very much and it was getting harder each week. I felt that, if I should telephone him, it might make him feel obliged to come to see me if he did not really want to. So all I could do was to leave the door open, and continue packing my memories into boxes, some of which I knew I might never open again myself.

Chapter Sixteen

Fridays were long days, and as I finished work at the manor to drive over to Madam's at "Kingston", I usually arrived between 6 o'clock and half past. She liked the company, and was very grateful about the flowers. The round of sandwiches and glass of non-alcoholic wine that Madam supplied me with, in the potting shed, meant that I didn't have to make tea when I got home, and so I was usually retired by 10.30 p.m.

Nearing the end of November I had to telephone Helen over a legal matter, which gave me the opportunity to enquire about Dale. It became evident that any time I attempted to chastise Dale, he would make the decision not to contact me for long periods, which I felt was very unfair. When I asked his mum if she ever had to chastise him, she answered,' Yes'. For any father in such a situation it was a tormenting time, as when Dale was only with me for a day, it was important to overcome any obstacles and move on with a lighter note before it was time for him to leave. This was something I had to learn to perfect, whilst being very aware that Dale, like most children, was playing one parent against the other to avoid discipline. Not knowing what Dale's relationship was like with his mum's husband meant that I had to try and read between the lines, obviously trying to avoid any unnecessary stress for Dale, whilst not wanting him to have all his own way.

With Christmas only weeks away, I knew this was going to be a hard time, so I was making every effort to condition myself by keeping busy and getting lots of sleep. I knew that I must not let Dale play with my emotions, so I was preparing to lock his love away and get on with my life if he had chosen not to see me anymore. The very sad thing was that I knew it was not Dale's fault, and that he might, when he became an adult, find certain times very difficult. I kept his key fob with me always (he had made it for me at school) and hoped that he would never forget the love that I have for him.

The past week had seen me get ahead with many extra jobs and even begin a project at work.

Sunday morning saw a reasonably early start. I collected mum at 10.30 a.m. on the way back from Rita and Gordon's, where I had just collected some boxes they had saved me from the pet shop for packing. As usual, they asked me to join them up in the Cragg Valley for tea, but I declined, insisting that packing was priority now.

As each box was completed, mum taped it up, whilst I numbered it and checked my list of contents. I hadn't worked closely with mum on anything for years now: now I remembered how we used to help her decorate houses and make gardens every few years when she felt the urge to move. Even at seventy, she still had what she referred to as "pluck" and "staying power" when it came to getting a job done. But I had noticed how much she was smoking and was aware of her anxiety over my situation, both in moving house and with Dale's absence, so I tried to slow the pace without making it obvious, as she would have hated to have felt inadequate.

We had lunch and a few breaks, chatting and reminiscing. I know I have been a stubborn character over the years and could sense mum trying to teach me the "softly, softly" approach with Dale. She was right, and I knew I must try hard not to dwell on my situation and keep smiling if I wanted my relationship with my son to survive.

After finishing the last big pack indoors, I asked mum if she felt up to beginning the loft. With her sarcastic remark about my "magpie-like" habits, we both reacted with a smile, as she showed her eagerness to begin another session. As I handed down each piece through the manhole, she pretended to be speechless at my hoarding, eventually expressing her amazement. Mum has little regard for anything that is not in use. Many a time while growing up I had witnessed her disposing of valuable items in an instant.

At 9.30 p.m. we marked up box number 32. There was just Dale's bedroom now and one cupboard in the kitchen. I suggested to mum that we leave them until next weekend. It was getting hard now towards the end and I tried to restrain any emotion as I sensed mum's concern.

We discussed briefly what I might do with the furniture, canary, rabbit and Smudge, should I not get another house in time before moving out. For all our disagreements over the years, mum has always left the door open to us all should we be in any difficulty, and here again, she put forward with all sincerity her offer to accommodate me lock, stock and barrel, no matter what hardship she caused herself. She knew I was grateful, but I could not see her coping at this age with my huge predicament and so I knew I must try as hard as I could to get through somehow.

Mum had enquired whether Dale had been in touch and so I showed her a one-line letter, which his mum had sent by post on Saturday morning, saying that Dale was not coming that Sunday. I had found it particularly difficult to face anyone or indeed the rest of the weekend. It had been six weeks now since his half-term holiday and he would not 'phone me. I really didn't know why Dale had taken such a stance, and asked his mum to encourage him to visit me, but she would not. I just had to try as I might to go on and keep busy.

After taking mum home, I prepared for work on Monday, and was in bed by midnight, exhausted.

On Sunday, 5th December 1999, mum and I found quite a few more things to pack in my bedroom, so did not manage to begin Dale's room. Smudge sat by Dale's bedroom door and began purring and meowing. She was a smart cat and always knew that at weekends I would allow Dale to let her into his bedroom, where she would curl up on the blue blanket on his bed whilst he smothered her with affection. So I let her in, but it was sad to see her looking for him. She settled down on his blanket, as mum and I looked on knowing next weekend we would have to pack up Dale's bedroom.

There was still no contact from Dale and with Christmas approaching, I decided to make one last effort by writing a letter to him, which I asked to be passed to him at his school. If he really did not wish to see me again, I did not want him to feel obliged to come against his wishes. So, I just let him know that I still loved him, and hoped that, whatever he did decide to do, he would be happy.

On Tuesday, 14th December, I had, as usual, after shutting the garden gate, checked the postbox. There, in between the rest of the mail, was an envelope I was most anxious to receive – it had Dale's writing on it. A mixture of relief and excitement ran through me, then, for a few awful moments, I wondered how I would cope if he had decided not to see me anymore. I had to open it; there was no one else to do so. The most joyful feeling came over me as I read his words: *'I would like to see you again Dad! I will come on Sunday 19th at 10.30 a.m. Love you. Dale x.'*

I read the letter over again before Sunday and made sure that I was ready on time. The doorbell rang and Dale came in. As he looked at me he was white, as though he'd been under some strain. He clung to me, resting his head on my chest with sheer relief. We hugged, as I enquired if he was alright. In that short time of not seeing him for eight weeks, which seemed much longer to me, he had grown and slimmed down. I did not question why he had gone so long without contacting me, or where he had been for his half-term holiday, I just knew he was happy and that was all that mattered. He will probably tell me in his own time.

After a short while he enquired about the house move, seeing all the boxes packed up. I couldn't tell him too much due to the delay with solicitors, but just that it could happen at any time. I suggested that we go out for lunch since the house was bare and untidy. He readily agreed, and so we spent the most beautiful afternoon in Haworth.

We arrived home for 6.00 p.m., had tea, and chatted until his mum came to collect him at 7.45 p.m. I was pleasantly surprised when he told me that he had made his Christmas plans to come and stay with me on Christmas Eve and return to his mum about 4.00 p.m. on Christmas Day. I did check to see if his mum approved, which he told me she did. We said our goodbyes, which, thankfully, were for only a few days.

Most of my life I have found it relatively easy to accept change, except in major situations such as bereavement or, I suppose, anything which saddens me. For the four and a half years since Helen and Dale had left me I had certainly resented change of any kind, finding it difficult to adjust to the smallest things. Only in the last six months had I, with the help of a few very loyal friends, and mum, been able to accept that there was hope to go forward once again and build on new foundations.

The only way I knew how to cope was to become insular, gradually clearing up the debris of a broken marriage, home and family. Trying to tie up loose ends and making sense of myself and life had left me exhausted. I am very lucky, and remain extremely grateful to my mother and grandparents, for the way they ingrained in me the importance of a good night's sleep, prayer, and good wholesome food. So, hopefully, I could now continue to sustain body and soul and once again look forward to the future.

Although I may never understand, or be able to make sense of what happened to my marriage, I felt some pride in that I had dealt with it alone and not inflicted my sadness on another partner. The future was for me to continue building on my career in horticulture and to establish myself in another house. However, one thing inside me remained unresolved; I felt that I should never be able to call a house my home again. As they say: "home is where the heart is", and my heart was with my family – Helen and Dale. A soul mate may only be found once in a lifetime.

On Friday, 24th December 1999, Christmas Eve, Dale arrived at 7.00 p.m. prompt. He was in good spirits and brought a warm glow from within me. He couldn't wait to give me my Christmas card and present – two small, neatly wrapped packages. *'What are we doing dad?'* he enquired, not letting the bareness of the house dampen his Christmas spirits. We went downstairs. There was no Christmas tree to put the presents around as usual, but with great expectation Dale asked where the presents were. I was so pleased to be able to direct him to a box in my bedroom, which had steadily filled with presents from some very kind friends and family for both Dale and me over the last few weeks. Shrieks of excitement filled the house as he brought the box downstairs. He amazed me by finding the enthusiasm to display all the presents around the front of the dresser. The house suddenly came to life as he began standing up all the cards, which I had not been able to bring myself to do. He begged me to open the presents; I resisted as always, which I was sure that he would appreciate, if not then, in years to come – that patience must prevail. *'Christmas Day and not before,'* I insisted, as he felt his way around each present with all the excitement a parent could wish to see on a child's face. He was uncontrollable with excitement and fidgeted, switching the television from station to station.

Eventually, after our supper, he took me by complete surprise by asking if I would like to go to a carol service. At first I declined, explaining that Midnight Mass would be too late for him, and we should perhaps go to bed. He knew how much I liked carol services and seemed sensitive and very thoughtful, asking a second time to go. It was some years since I had been and it was nice to see Dale interested, so we called in at Nanna Laura's on the way to deliver her Christmas card and present. She was pleased to see him and as we chatted, her next-door friend, Margaret, showed interest in going with Dale and me to Haworth's Midnight Mass.

We arrived at Haworth by 11.05 p.m. As we walked up the main cobbled street, Dale pointed out all the shops we had visited the previous Sunday. Lights twinkled from trees and out of houses all the way up to the church. We were warmly welcomed, took our places in the pew, and continued to enjoy the service lit by dozens of candles. Dale was nothing short of admirable for a twelve year old. There was only another one of similar age in the congregation and, as we approached the final carol at 12.35 a.m., Dale was holding on to the front pew with eyes half closed and rocking on his feet. He had made the offer with all sincerity, not realising how tired he would become.

Once we returned to the van, he fell asleep in the back. We dropped mum's neighbour off at home and arrived home ourselves at 1.15 a.m. I filled Dale's hot water bottle and watched him drift cosily asleep. It took me another hour downstairs just tidying up little things before eventually taking myself to bed.

At 8.00 a.m. on Christmas Day I was awakened by a voice sleepily beckoning me downstairs. *'Come on dad, dad come on.'* No matter how tired I was, those words meant the world to me. This was his moment. We both wrapped ourselves in a duvet and squatted down in front of the dresser. Dale insisted we opened each other's gift first. A broad smile crept across my face as I opened a jar of the finest pink grapefruit marmalade by Crabtree & Evelyn, and a sheep in a type of resin to add to the collection of animals which Dale had bought me on other occasions. I watched closely for Dale's reaction as he opened his present from me. Thank goodness it was alright. *'Dad, it's brilliant, thanks.'* It was a fleece top he had tried on in my friend Tony's sports shop in the summer and very much liked. After we'd finished opening the presents, I put Dale's into a cardboard box so that he could take them with him.

We were invited down to Rita and Gordon's for Christmas lunch at 2.00 p.m. and then Dale's mum called to collect him at 4.00 p.m. I waved him off, as he proudly walked down the road wearing his new top and holding his box of presents. It was to be a week on Sunday before I would see him again. He had made plans to go to his friend Julian's for New Year's Eve, to have a firework party for the Millennium. I couldn't help but think inside that he should be with his parents at this young age, but Dale couldn't help this, and thankfully was making the most of things. I just hoped that he would be in good hands.

That evening I stayed behind with Rita and Gordon for supper, chatting and lazily watching television until almost midnight. They had made a wonderful effort to accommodate Dale and myself and had put on a lovely lunch. I bid them both *'Goodnight'* and drove home.

The festive season was a long stretch that year, with Christmas Day falling on Saturday and additional holidays for the Millennium.

My employers had invited me to the manor for Boxing Day 1999 at 1.00 p.m. So that morning, after a lazy start, I completed chores and drove over. They gave me their usual warm welcome and fixed bacon and egg sandwiches whilst we chatted into the afternoon. Then their daughter and boyfriend arrived with his friend and tea was served. A lovely cold sit down buffet in the dining room, all laid complete with Christmas crackers. We then returned to the lounge, playing a game to which introduced us all. Then I left to make my journey back over Cockhill Moor to Hebden Bridge, arriving home just before midnight.

My next invitation was to "Penfold Cottage", near Ullswater in The Lake District, with my friends Tony and Mary.

On Monday, 27th December 1999 it was lovely once again to waken gradually with no alarm at 9.30 a.m. I had left it too late to book Smudge into the cattery, and as I was only going to be away for one night, decided she would go with me and stay in the van; she was very much used to riding in it. So cat litter tray, carrier, food, toys and hot water bottle were all in addition to my overnight bag, oh, and of course, Smudge. We left at 2.00 p.m., filling up with diesel en route, and arrived at "Penfold Cottage" at 5.00 p.m. on a very frosty evening with a covering of snow, to find Tony and Mary busying themselves in the kitchen.

After a merry greeting, I dived in with a helping hand, as Tony's brother, Charles and his wife and daughter, and Tony's sister, Bev, were joining us for an evening meal. The table looked inviting, not to mention the food, and the evening stretched out over a couple of games of Trivial Pursuit.

Next morning I joined Tony and Mary for breakfast at 9.00 a.m. After that, Tony left to open his shop in Appleby for the sale. I took myself off over the fells, calling at John and Margaret's, the people I had farmed for nearly twenty years before and whom I had met through Tony and with whom I had remained friendly ever since. Then on to drop a cheque in at a tree nursery before stopping off at Tony's shop, where we always seem to manage to recall a few of our sporting days together.

I should have been travelling back that evening as I was due back at work on the Wednesday, but Tony and Mary insisted that I stay and said that they would wake me in time on Wednesday morning to travel straight to work. We had another very pleasant evening and retired by 9.00 p.m., ready for an early start. The following morning, Tony left for milking at 4.30 a.m. and I was not far behind at 5.00 a.m., leaving behind a clear half moon and a sky full of stars shining over snow-covered fells, as I headed towards the M6. Smudge travelled very well and stayed in the van whilst I worked on Wednesday.

It had been a lovely Christmas after all, I just had to try and forget that my home was all packed up in boxes. Friends had been so very kind, and it was so good to have seen Dale. However, I knew that the coming holiday for New Year 2000 was going to be very different, and braced myself for a much lonelier period.

Dale had told me that he was going to be with friends on New Year's Eve (Friday). I finished work at 4.30 p.m., leaving my employers getting ready for a night across the valley at friends. Arriving home, I worked my way through the evening's chores and took myself to bed by 7.20 p.m.

That night I awoke with such a bewildered feeling. It was pitch black as I stretched across to see what time it was, the clock read "12.03". Everything suddenly dawned, as I could hear bangs and flashes shone through into the bedroom. It was very unusual for even fireworks to wake me, because I was such a heavy sleeper, although I realised I had already had nearly five hours' sleep.

When there is a special occasion it is always nice to share it with someone special, so I knew I would find it difficult being alone for the Millennium and had hoped to sleep through. However, I drew back one curtain and sat on the edge of the bed watching as the celebrations lit up the length and breadth of the valley for the next three quarters of an hour. I could feel my mind wandering and emotions, which I had tried to avoid, creeping in. Eventually, by a quarter to one, the fireworks had finished and the main road began to get busy with traffic. I climbed back into bed and didn't know a thing more until 10.15 a.m.

On Saturday I lazily worked my way through the day and sat down to write. I could not remember a New Year's Day when I had not ventured outside, so at 3.00 p.m. I drove a mile up the main road just to see if there was any sign of life. But everywhere was deserted, so I returned home and continued writing before turning in for the night. Tomorrow was to look forward to – Dale was coming.

The most significant thing I did that day was to write in the date, the year "2000". It was such a strange feeling, as I am sure that it was for millions of others when they came to write it for the first time. Although there had been a great public build-up and climax to this date, I felt that it was only now that we really took on board that this was a timely reminder that nothing does stay the same.

It felt good to be settling back into my routine again at work after the New Year, and it was not long before I received a telephone call from my solicitor to discuss the buying and selling of houses.

I had hoped to be able to find a small cottage in the Skipton area, one that did not need much work doing to it so that I could move straight in, but that was not to be. All the small cottages were much sought after, with prices escalating by the day. It was the beginning of another housing boom and prices would soar, as they did in the eighties.

After over a year of searching, a most unexpected property presented itself as I drove past and noticed the "For Sale" sign. This was too good to be true. I reversed and took a good look. The farthest thing from my mind had been a semi-detached house, but this had an appeal to me. It was badly neglected, though a good solid stone house, and what's more, only three minutes by car from work, so I could walk if necessary. A further inspection with the estate agent revealed a lot of work, but at the right price it would be worth it.

With the help of one of my employers friends my bid was accepted and I began work. This would be ongoing for some years, as I would have to live in it whilst renovating it on a very low budget. Dale had been to see the house and was pleased. I was to move in on the 2nd February, 2000.

Chapter Seventeen

I had now worked at the manor for nearly three years, long enough for me to know that I was making the right move with my house. Throughout that time my employers had continued to show concern, and made every effort to help me settle in, so much so that they became friends, as much as could be expected in an employer/employee situation. I have to say that, although my nature allowed me to show my appreciation to them in many ways, I do feel that I may have come across as somewhat aloof at times. This side of me is a combination of shyness; my time spent in catering, where it was important not to become too familiar with customers; and the impact of my divorce, that had made it extremely difficult for me to trust anyone. I can only hope that this will never damage my friendship with my employers, who, I hope, have never taken offence at the time and effort they have put into trying to get to know me. I feel sure that my guard against human nature is gradually lowering, although never completely dropped, and hope that faith will be somewhat restored.

Their kindness extended to their asking their son to take on my house removal, which he duly did, lock, stock and barrel, with his Land Rover and cattle trailer in three journeys.

I had come a long way now over the last five years, albeit at a slow pace. Almost every day in my work along the way I would dig. This would be either digging a hole for planting, removing rocks, turning the vegetable garden, or merely weeding; but every day my garden spade would heal my hurts. I could now, at last, feel things gathering pace, although the legal side of moving would drag on for the rest of the year.

By the end of the year I was to realise that I had almost missed the boat, as house prices soared, but here I was at last, only walking distance from work, a few miles from Skipton and the Yorkshire Dales, and above all, within easy distance to see my son and mum.

The house was little more than a shell as I knocked down walls, re-wired, re-did the plumbing, and began putting it back together with the vision I had for it. I could see its potential, which helped me to cope with the very basic living conditions. But my heart felt for Dale, who never once complained and continued to come and bring his friends.

My first purchases were a fridge, a cooker, and a washer, making sure that Dale had a clean bed and good food on all his visits. The van continued to give us many memorable outings; long beyond the six months I had anticipated with its rusting bodywork. After nearly two years and a few pools of water in the front, I knew it was no longer safe to be on the road, so in the October of 2001 I was once again without transport. But this time I was prepared. A good pair of shoes and a winter coat provided by my friend Tony helped me brave the elements as I walked to and from work. Both Dale and I were making an extra effort to keep in contact now by means of buses, taxis and trains. This would bring some sense of adventure to Dale's journeys, as he was now fourteen years old and found this a good opportunity to begin to gain some independence.

However, as every parent will know, the teenage years can be perilous, and as much as I meant what I thought to myself at that vulnerable time of my own life – that I would not worry about my children the way mum did about us all – only then could I take on board what she must have felt, as I gradually became aware of some of Dale's vulnerable situations.

Fortunately, Dale was honest in telling me some of the places he went with his friends. I could feel the alarm bells ringing, as his explorings were a world away from mine at his age, and with a high element of danger. I can only think that he was sensible enough to realise this as I somehow found a way of having heart-to-heart chats with him, whilst trying not to come across too heavily. I could sense that he needed me there to try and keep him safe, but without his friends knowing. It is so very agonising, standing on the sidelines and wondering if your child is going to be one of the casualties or even fatalities that makes the papers. Looking back to the day he was born, I am only too aware of how secretly protective I have become of him over the years, even more so since my role had to be carried out from a distance.

Throughout my school years, I was a solitary child, enjoying my grandparents' country life-style, and not opting for the more daring things that would attract my peers. It made me a perfect target for some of the cruelties of which children are capable in schools, and had it not been for my elder brother's reputation as "a tough character", I may have come off much worse. So, either way, the hard fact is that life does not offer us a guarantee that our children will come through unscathed. A weapon, which Dale handed to me and agreed I could destroy in front of him, remains a terrifying reminder and testimony of how very close he came to danger in his early teens. I would count my blessings each time I saw him, and still do. I felt I had saved him from harm. A feeling all parents want to experience, but whether a child is from parents who are divorced or together, inevitably they have to encounter life's dangers at some time. For me, being unable to see Dale on a daily basis just makes that parent pain barrier much more painful to deal with.

I once read an article that said, *"No precipice is so attractive as one that has a terrified parent waving from the lip of it, hectoring you to stay away from the edge."* Of course, as they grow, this effort continues. I would not want to embarrass Dale by revealing my anxiety for his safety, as this might cause him to be ashamed of me. So I try to perfect coping with those feelings, whilst at the same time trying to be there as a "safety net".

When I look at Dale, I often imagine how my dad must have felt in his fight to keep me. That fierce hurt that Dale will not encounter until he has children of his own. I only hope I can be there to help Dale should he need me. As for me, I had no choice; it was mum who was there.

(Sunday, 6th June 2004. As you will gather from this date, I am now into my fourth year of renovating my house. Progress is slow due to the difficulty in getting workmen – a problem everyone I speak to seems to have. It is a very busy period at work, and as I try to keep up with domestic chores, it leaves me little time to continue writing.

Mum is extremely helpful, both financially and morally. I could not have achieved things as quickly as I have this year without her help, for which she knows I am forever grateful. But this brings certain drawbacks, as mum finds it increasingly difficult being alone as the years go by, and so constantly turns to Sandra and me on a daily basis for contact by telephone, or to be with her for company. This weekend has left me feeling somewhat guilty, as I gave her an excuse on the telephone in order to have it to myself and once again indulge in my secret writing of this book.)

It was important now that I recognised how fast Dale was achieving independence, and that, because he lived with his mum, I would inevitably see less of him as time went by. I could only hope that the time we had given each other would remain as precious to him as it does to me. I will not let my love for Dale turn to resentment as he goes on to build a life of his own, though I dearly hope that he will keep in touch. The need for me to fill another empty space in my life had now dawned.

Although my daily walks to and from work were only twenty-five minutes each way, I found the evenings had quickly escaped me by the time I had prepared myself for the next day. So, noticing cyclists were passing me by on their way home, I decided to save up and get myself a push-bike. By May 2002, I had saved enough to buy a secondhand bike, which had taken my liking, at a cost of £300. It was a huge expense and a big decision at the time, but one I knew I needed to make if I was going to make progress.

I had dearly loved my fell running days, but knew the best were firmly behind me, and dare not attempt to begin again for fear of injury jeopardising my work. Each weekend, dozens of cyclists from local clubs would pass my house en route to The Dales, so my reason for taking up cycling was threefold: one, to cut down on time to and from work; two, it would cut out the running costs of a vehicle, which were out of the question; and three, it was a chance to meet people.

This was a real breath of fresh air to me, as I gradually bought accessories and clothing throughout that year. I was encouraged to become a member of a local cycling club with which I began weekend rides around The Dales. This initially came as a shock as I realised how much fitness I had lost since my fell running days. However, I persevered and eventually became able to keep up with the pack.

At this point I detected some surprise, if not concern, in Dale's reaction to my activities, almost as though he thought that I should not move on, or was incapable of moving on with my life as he was with his. I felt sad that he did not show happiness for me moving on with my life the way that I was happy for him to do so. Maybe he was finding it difficult to understand that this did not mean that I felt any less of him.

Throughout that year we continued to have good times together, playing squash, swimming, shopping, and hiring a car to travel up to Tony and Mary's and doing other day trips together. Somehow, I could sense these times were coming to an end, as Dale's school work was playing a bigger part in the way he was to begin to shape his future. However, we still managed to spend part of Christmas together.

In May 2003 Dale had arranged to meet me in Halifax for a game of squash. My bus journey got me there half an hour early but after I had waited an hour, Dale finally 'phoned me, reluctant to admit that he was still in bed after a late night with his friends. I was initially annoyed, but knew he was finding it difficult now to find time to fit me into his life. I had already accepted this, and so made my bus journey back home, knowing there would be no more games of squash, and that I could only try to be there for him in whatever capacity I was needed.

From that day, communications broke down and after four months and an effort on mum's part, we finally contacted each other, which was a great relief to us both.

During that year, mum had found it increasingly difficult to maintain her house and was making plans to sell it and move into a flat in the valley, near to one of my sisters. This was partly brought about by feeling the need to help my other sister, Sandra, financially, due to her becoming homeless. There was a lot of pressure on mum, and eventually, after us all helping her to move, by the 24th September 2003, she spent her first night in her new flat.

Over the last few years, mum had come to see her visits to me as little holidays, as she would either catch the bus over with her overnight bag, or Sandra would bring her in her car. She looked forward to this as a complete change from any anxieties through her and Sandra's relationship. She often mentioned though how troubled she was that I did not have any transport, and if she needed me urgently, that I could not get over to her.

On one visit in September, after selling her house, mum declared that, as she had shared some of her money between my other brothers and sisters, she would like to buy me a car. We made a short journey to a secondhand garage in Skipton, and true to form mum, as impulsive as ever, bought me a car, of which I am so very proud; I enjoy the luxury of having it. It has given us both peace of mind as well as much pleasure.

Dale's half-term holiday from school was the next month and he had agreed to spend some days with me, which I was so excited about now that I had a car. As he did not have any idea what to do or where he wanted to go, I made plans for a few days in Northumberland as a change from The Lake District.

Before the holiday even began, we had the sad experience of having to take Dale's cat Smudge to the vet to be put to sleep after a tragic accident had left her badly injured. Dale seemed to cope with the situation very well, not showing any emotion, whilst I struggled to fight back the tears and continue with the holiday. We went on to enjoy the most beautiful weather and scenery, but knowing this would probably be our last holiday together. It was a far cry from the exotic holiday his mum and her husband had taken him on a few months earlier to Sri Lanka, and I was left with the feeling that my effort never really came up to the standard of living Dale had with his mum and her husband.

Yet again, though my house was still very basic and in the ongoing state of refurbishment, Dale came and spent Christmas with me.

Unfortunately, on the run up to Christmas, mum was taken ill with shingles. This had been brought on with the trauma of moving house and the stress of Sandra's domestic situation. We all did what we could to help her through and fortunately, in the weeks and months after, mum made a good recovery. She had financed Sandra, enabling her to buy a house, into which Sandra had now moved and begun work on, at the same time as starting a new relationship.

The year 2003 had been an eventful one, presenting many changes within the family, but however difficult we may have found them, mum's unwavering tenacity as a guardian still at the helm, who does not want to let go, who will not let go until her final day, makes me wonder how difficult she had found it over the years as she has had to watch on. This makes me wonder even more if I will ever be as strong.

Dale's stay with me that Christmas was short, as he had arranged to stay with me on Christmas Eve and return to his mum and her husband at 1.00 p.m. on Christmas Day. But it was always nice to give him a Christmas meal.

(It is now 13th June 2004, and Dale has not visited me since Christmas Day.)

Early in January, when mum was suffering badly with the shingles, she had lost weight, could not keep food down, and complained of being depressed. It was very obvious to me what was happening, though we were all limited as to what we could do because mum is so very independent. She eventually told me that she had not wanted to move into the flat. This was a very backward step for mum; she had been so very active and forward looking and had always lived in her own home. The reality of no longer having her own home had suddenly struck her, and thrown her into depression, subsequently triggering shingles; she had also taken a fall from standing on a chair. The combination of these events, and constant fallouts with Sandra over her lifestyle, had taken their toll and left mum more exhausted than I had ever seen her before. Mum's relationship with my other sister, who lived close by, was very frosty. She was now feeling very neglected and going downhill fast, as she struggled alone with only visits from the doctor.

I drove over from work with supplies and checked on her until she began to improve. Eventually, on 10th January she was able to come and stay the weekend with me, but she was finding her recovery difficult, still bearing the pain of shingles and speaking of a lack of confidence, something that concerned me.

Sandra came to take her back the next day, but by the Wednesday mum 'phoned me at work to say that she was on the bus coming over to stay again. She was desperate for company, and fighting hard to shake off her depression, so whilst she stayed until the following Sunday, I took her out for meals and shopping.

She found it very difficult to cope with her financial duties from the sale of the house, confiding in me, which resulted in many discussions with my sisters, who agreed to my keeping a file of her documents, giving mum peace of mind. She was now speaking of transferring to another flat, as she was finding her present one too small and mum has always suffered with claustrophobia.

Although this came as a shock to us all, wondering how she would cope with another move so soon, I was determined to do everything I could to help her to be where she wanted at this time of her life. So, between us all, we made contacts, filled in forms and began the process of applying for a larger flat for mum. By now, Paula was helping more and making regular contact with mum. I made daily 'phone calls to keep her cheerful, and of course, give her hope, which she had always given us at our lowest points in life.

One evening in early February, sounding very low, mum 'phoned me. Paula and her husband were in Somerset visiting my elder brother and his wife, and mum was still not on speaking terms with Sandra. I drove the twenty miles to pick her up, and she stayed with me for ten days.

Gradually, she began to show signs of improving as she cleaned the house for me, went for bus rides whilst I was at work, and generally enjoyed herself. It is so sad that her happy times are always tainted by feeling the need to complain about either one of us. However, it was such a relief to see her looking so well again, and she was now feeling ready to go back, as I assured her of not having to stay the rest of her life in that small flat. She had been hurt that Sandra had not 'phoned her over the last ten days, but I knew that they would both need time, as they had both been under so much stress, and so I felt that I had been able to help, which was satisfying.

(11th March, 2004. The wind has been in the east for some four or five days now, bringing with it flurries of snow, but not sufficient to show white on the ground. I have increased my layers again. With no heat in the potting shed, gaping holes and the deterioration of the greenhouse, it is too cold and damp to stand still and sow my seed, so I brace myself and find a job that keeps me moving outside.)

A heavy project I had been working on alone for the past twelve months at work had come to an end in mid-March, leaving me feeling low enough to pick up a viral infection which, to my amazement, took me off my legs, leaving me bed-bound for a week. As I was in daily contact with mum, she inevitably found out about my condition and was at the helm until I was able to return to work. This was the role she thrived on – tending to any one of us at times of illness – but finding it very difficult if the situation was reversed.

Living alone, I am only too aware of the difficulties illness can cause, and so make every effort to take care of myself. Unfortunately, on this occasion, work got the better of me, but it was good to be up and about again. I gave mum her Mother's Day present, thanked her for her help, and drove her home.

I had spoken to Dale earlier and arranged to take him for lunch. So, after dropping mum off, I went on to pick him up. The figure that walked towards the car filled me with worry, sadness and sickness. This was the first time Dale had let me visit him since Christmas. In that time he had shot up almost, it seemed, to just short of six foot. But he was gaunt, looked unhappy and had lost so much weight that I could see every bone in his body.

He sat beside me as we greeted each other. My usual words of, *'Are you alright?'* seemed feeble, as I could clearly see that he was not, but knew that I had to tread carefully. It was difficult, very difficult to know what to say. My son, whom I dearly loved and whom I had always encouraged to look after his body, was struggling, and I didn't know why. All I wanted to do was help, but he seemed to want to keep me at a distance.

We drove half an hour over the moors to Hebden Bridge, and in that time, thankfully, he began to open up. A combination of deciding to give up his 'A' level studies; doing a part-time job, which he did not like; his mum changing her job; not eating a balanced diet; and being short of sleep were things that he had been bottling up. I was just so glad to let him pour it all out and to be there for him. However, when I mentioned his weight loss, he became annoyed, saying that he felt fine and that his mum never mentioned his weight. Maybe I was being paranoid, but when we arrived at our café, he was unable to eat anything more than a sandwich and a Coke. This, to me, seemed unhealthy for a growing seventeen year old, and knowing the meals he had eaten when I cooked for him, but I had to leave the subject so as not to make him feel uncomfortable. I just hoped that he could sense my concern.

He became at ease when he realised that I was not annoyed at him dropping out of school, and went on to tell me of his plans to take up an electrical apprenticeship; I was thrilled about this and encouraged him to look forward.

He asked to visit his Nanna Laura. They were so pleased to see each other, and after a chat, I drove him back to his mum's. There was no doubt that he had lost his way in life and was trying to find some direction. I could only hope that our time together had helped him to get back on the right track, and that he would contact me if ever he was finding life difficult.

In early April I treated mum and Dale to lunch at a restaurant on the outskirts of Halifax, which we all enjoyed. Throughout our lives, mum had never been able to give either of us a birthday party, so when she pointed out that I would be fifty that year, and she would like to take me out for a meal, I was, to say the least, surprised. She booked a table there and then for Saturday, 1st May, because Sandra,

Dale and Paula's birthdays were all very close too, and she thought it would be a good idea to swell the numbers to include them, along with Sandra's new man friend. This made me feel somewhat uneasy, but I let mum go ahead with the arrangements as I knew her of old, and that this would be a good excuse to get the whole family together.

Well, the 1st May arrived, and I drove over to collect mum and Sandra's two girls and Dale for 11.30 a.m. We arrived in plenty of time for our 12.30 p.m. lunch. On entering the bar area, there, to my sheer astonishment, was my elder brother Larry from Somerset, with his wife. I greeted them and readily thanked them for making the effort to come up. Mum had arranged everything, unbeknown to me, and pleaded with them to make the journey, for which she had paid. She had taken great pains to be able to bring us all together. She herself enjoyed the day very much, which was a pleasure to see. My younger brother, Darren, was also there, but for all her dogged determination to have her own way at organising things, I could not help but feel sorry for her as her numerous attempts at inviting my sister Paula had been rejected. Paula said that she was not into birthdays, and so did not come.

I was overwhelmed at the lovely family cards and presents I received, and could easily have shown a tear, but managed to compose myself and enjoy the happy event. Yes, mum, it was a wonderful day and one I shall never forget. Thank you for your great efforts.

Chapter Eighteen

My birthday celebrations had extended over the following week, as I took up Tony and Mary's offer to take me out for a meal. After driving mum and Dale back home, I made the journey up to "Penfold Cottage", where I stayed until Monday. Mary was fully engrossed in midwifery, as she was in the middle of lambing her flock of Herdwicks, so Tony and I lunched in idyllic surroundings in a hotel on the edge of Ullswater.

The following weekend saw me dining out yet again, this time with my friends Rita and Gordon at one of their local haunts on the outskirts of Halifax.

My life had always revolved around helping and arranging things for people, which I had grown accustomed to: helping mum with my brothers and sisters until I left home; taking care of livestock during my farming years; preparing and hosting endless functions throughout my time in catering; and eventually tending the many gardens and plants which gave me and others so much pleasure. Though I felt that I tried, it is not for me to comment on my marriage due to the outcome, but for all the efforts I had made, it was as though God was now rewarding me through family and friends, at a time which seemed to me just like any other birthday. I am left only to say that I was very humbled that this small number of people had remained close to me after the many burdens I had laid at their doorsteps over my recent troubled years.

(It is now Sunday, 20th June 2004, and as I write at very

close to midnight, it brings me ever closer to completing this, my final chapter.)

Major external works to the house were coming to an end, which would allow me to continue with the inside and, hopefully, begin the garden.

Mum was in good health and feeling optimistic about a flat transfer. We spoke every day by telephone, and she loved to come and visit. With much persuasion from Larry, his wife and me, along with her own courage, mum had finally decided to take a week's holiday with Larry and his wife in Somerset the next month. I just hoped that she would be able to relax and enjoy her time there; she was more than overdue for a treat.

After sending my "thank you" cards for my birthday presents, I realised that that would probably be the last contact I would have with Larry and Darren until Christmas greetings were exchanged. Despite all the visits I had made to Paula through mum's requests and arrangements, as well as my own, for some reason Paula did not reciprocate. However, whether friends or family, people choose their company. Sandra appeared to be settling into her new home and relationship, and liked to contact me by 'phone whenever she could, though life with her two girls was now quite hectic.

With no 'phone call from Dale to wish me 'happy birthday', and a message left on the answer machine wishing me *'happy birthday'* on Father's Day, I realised that I was becoming a more distant figure to him.

(9.20 p.m. – Wednesday, 20th October, 2004. If I only write the time and date at this point, it will be sufficient to release some of the frustration that has built up inside me since I was last able to write back in June. The challenge of keeping this book a secret is becoming almost unbearable, as I struggle for time to pick up my pen knowing that, as the end nears, I shall at last be able to make plans to have it printed. As this year has progressed, time has been very much of the essence, with many events taking priority over my writing.)

Mum had been very thoughtful and generous by way of giving each of us a sum of money after the sale of her house, initially helping Sandra with the purchase of hers. Mum was quite happy for me to spend mine on the development of my house, so what was originally a longer-term plan for a workshop and coal store, went ahead much more quickly and has now been completed; giving both mum and myself great satisfaction.

With Dale now in his late teens, I understood that his time was very much taken up with friends, college, and part-time work. However, I did have difficulty in understanding why he continued to go for long spells without telephoning. If I then made a 'phone call, he could be very abrupt and disinterested in me, so I just had to leave him to it. I somehow managed to learn to cope with this situation without getting too upset.

I had made a special effort, and managed to make visits to three "open gardens" in 2004 over the weekends. This I had found completely transported me away from any family difficulties, lifting my spirits and keeping me whole.

After much correspondence, through letters and 'phone calls, mum eventually got a transfer and moved into her new flat on Saturday, 7th August 2004. She was eager for us all to see it, so I drove over the following day for her to show me around. She could hardly contain her excitement, and afterwards agreed to a drive over to Skipton, where we had lunch and shopped, before I took her back home.

She requested many more outings in the following weeks, ordering and collecting new furniture, buying plants for me to create a small garden, as well as attending financial appointments.

With regular telephone calls, keeping me informed of her decorating, I tried to persuade her to have a decorator, but she insisted on doing it herself. I became alarmed, knowing that she had taken a bad fall from standing on a chair at the previous flat, and so drove over to check on her.

However, I knew if I were to show concern, this would be interpreted as ridiculing her, and her feisty defiance was instantly recognisable, as she swiftly and proudly showed me from one room to the next, where not a square inch had escaped her paintbrush.

It was almost inconceivable that, less than six months ago, she had been brought so low with illness and depression, and now this slight figure before me, at seventy-five years of age, was exuding once again "her will to do".

My last garden visit in 2004 was on Friday, 24th September, and was in complete contrast to my first back in May. A rugged landscape, yet interestingly diverse and set high in the Northumbrian hills, "Craggside" had risen, and was still rising to many challenges. The day left me fulfilled, inspired, and content that I am a gardener.

The journey to "Craggside" had taken me, for the most part, on a route which Dale and I had taken last October for his half-term holiday. This allowed me to reflect on some of my precious memories and time spent with my son.

Although I have had to condition myself to travelling alone over the years, it still does not come easily. On this occasion, I made the effort to stay overnight at North Shields with my friend Jan, whom I had not seen now for more than ten years. We had spoken by telephone a couple of times a year, but to meet her again was a treat. The following morning provided us with a pleasant walk on the seafront, as we discussed "memory lane" and caught up with present times, whilst calling in for coffee and cakes.

By 3.00 p.m. I waved goodbye to Jan and drove over to "Penfold Cottage", where I had arranged to see Tony and Mary. Although Tony and I realise that there may be many things that we do not have in common, we are all too well aware of the interests that we share. Tony, himself a workaholic, though too modest to admit it, hit on hard times as a boy. It is this common ground that we can both empathise with that has steadily allowed our friendship to grow over the years. For all my beliefs that keep me strong, I never feel as weak as when I am in his company, as he unwaveringly tackles his next goal, unquestioning of any difficulty that may lie ahead. Whilst serving his time as a herdsman on a dairy farm, he also built up his own business in a sports shop. His hard work and kind nature have seen a strong local support, resulting in a job well done.

It was to this shop where, over the years, I would call with Dale whilst visiting The Lakes, when Tony's generous nature allowed me to be involved in many activities with Dale.

After seeing him suffer the loss of his first wife, I have watched him too rebuild his life. He began a relationship with someone he had known for many years; this gradually blossomed, and he informed me that they were to be married on 21st July, 2001. The wedding and reception took place at the "Sharrow Bay Hotel" on Ullswater, famously renowned for its cuisine. I was invited, and shall always hold dear to me a beautiful experience shared with a great friend.

His new wife, Mary, another seasoned workaholic, had welcomed me into her fold with all the warmth and hospitality known to a Cumbrian. I have since watched Tony's life move on in many ways. He has now sold his business, has settled into life on Mary's farm at "Penfold Cottage", and enjoys frequent holidays.

As I approached "Penfold" from leaving my friend Jan on the Saturday, it was almost 6.00 p.m. A few yards from the farm was a barn, from which Tony emerged, spade in hand and a gleeful expression on his face as he caught sight of my car pulling up. He waved me over and proceeded to explain how he was tackling his next goal. It was a barn conversion he was labouring on as part of one of many projects he and Mary were undertaking.

My arrival seemed timely as he announced that Mary had tea ready, so we made our way in, and on greeting Mary, I enjoyed yet another stay over at "Penfold" in good

Tony and Mary on their wedding day at the Sharrow Bay Hotel Ullswater Sat 21st July 2001

Penfold Cottage, Dockray, which is Tony and Mary's home in the Lake District and where I have enjoyed many holidays, both with Dale and by myself. Gowbarrow Fell is on the right in the background which Dale and me once walked up.

company as we browsed over holiday photographs of their recent cruise.

The following lunchtime saw me leave behind, once again, somewhere that had been a part of me for so many years, and head towards home.

Over time I have built up a collection of keepsakes, which Dale has very thoughtfully given me as presents, either from his holidays, or for Christmas, birthdays and Father's Day. These I cherish with great affection. Although I have always done the same for Dale, though maybe in a more practical way, such as clothes and items for school, I feel it is much harder to gauge now as his choices become much more personal and we do not see each other as often. It was during my weekend away at "Craggside" that I suddenly realised that the time had come where he would find money more useful in being able to make his own choice. A time when I had to give up some control I had become used to.

For anyone reading, who, like myself, may be fearful of not doing the right thing at the right time for someone they dearly love, and who does not wish to hurt their affections; please do not despair. It is within the purpose of my writing this book that, once again, I may encourage you to embrace that time when it arrives – that time of "change".

As I mentioned earlier in my book, change can be particularly hurtful when it involves people, but whether people, things or places, it is inevitable that it affects us all at different stages and in different ways throughout our lives. It may seem to some that it was no real problem but, as I stood alone casting my eyes around the gift shop, my thoughts initially in turmoil, there was a peaceful inner voice. I knew at this point that I had to let go of something I had enjoyed doing for many years. Desperate not to damage our relationship, which was currently fragile due to the late teenage years, I left the shop. Once home, I posted Dale a cheque, along with a note. He had already gone several weeks without contacting me but, within a few days, he telephoned in good heart to thank me for his money. My prayers, once again, had been answered.

I feel that most single parents in my situation would have tussled with their thoughts at such a time. You will have noticed earlier in my book, as a child, and into my adulthood, my desire for stability. That desire remains no less, but I have learned, like most things in life, there is a balance, and when change presents itself, it is sensitivity that helps us to decide "when" and "how" to deal with either of these situations. It is not to say that the opportunity to buy my son a present may never arise again, but by giving up control over a situation, and embracing change, both through prayer and sensitivity, I have allowed us both to grow and move forward with our lives.

Things on the domestic scene had moved on quite fast in 2004, taking up much of my "out of work" time. However, I had never lost site of my goal, which was to be able to write the last chapter of my book before the end of the year. So, not having taken any holidays from work in 2004, and with three weeks owed, I had decided to take them at intervals between October and Christmas, when I hoped to be able to bring this final chapter to a close.

(It is now Thursday, 28th October, 2004. My holidays began on Tuesday and I have been writing each day. I must return to work on Monday before my next break in November so, as the colder air and darker days are upon us, I have lit my stove and fully immersed myself in my writing.)

Back in 1992, shortly after opening my florist shop, something quite significant happened, and looking back now, I would even say it was remarkable. One day, a group of half a dozen or so ladies came in to browse. I could hear lots of comments being passed to and fro. Then, as they prepared to leave, one lady approached me, saying that they had just been on a visit to a famous flower arranger's shop, which I knew very well and which was not too far away from me. I vividly recall the most inferior feeling for both myself and my product, though I handled the situation reasonably well by showing interest in the other party. The lady went on to say that she was a teacher in floral design and, although she liked my arrangements, had detected that there was something missing in my work. Ever willing to learn, I did not take offence as she offered me her card whilst telling me when she held her classes and encouraging me to go along.

My first thought after she had left my shop was of her touting for business. This could not have been further from the truth, as I was to discover. Once I had overcome my initial embarrassment about entering a ladies' workshop, my determination to improve on my skills took over, and I began a three-month course in Floral Design, held in a picturesque village just outside Harrogate.

The lady, with such a pleasant manner and softly spoken voice, was Val Roberts, the wife of a local artist. She was to reveal to me my shortcomings – the "elements" and "principles" of design. This was the basis of her teaching which, by the end of the course, I knew off by heart and which will stay with me forever. Little did she know that this teaching was a catalyst to an event that would change the course of my life, as I moved on to my full-time course at college with the confidence and knowledge of those "elements" and "principles", which I continue to apply throughout my work.

Working with the colours and textures of flowers and foliage was pleasant, but I found the indoors too restrictive, and felt the need for a greater challenge. I knew this was only part of a process that was necessary to lead me to my ultimate goal of designing a large garden. I was still only at the beginning of my journey, and not knowing what the outcome would be brought great frustration and financial pressure for both my family and me. Little did I know that I was going to have to suffer so much pain for my gain. To gain the work that would fulfil me, and that would –

satisfy my soul.

"It is a matter of neither time, nor size nor site, nor the geographical location, nor even the plants. All these are variables, playing greater or lesser roles. All good gardens have one thing in common – the gardener who envisages, creates and cares for them. Each person must visualise what he wants his garden to be. If it fulfils his needs and hopes, it is a good garden for him, although on purely aesthetic grounds it may leave something to be desired. What other people think is bound to vary. What should interest every gardener is whether he can hand down the verdict of a 'good' garden on his own handiwork."

(Jane Brown: "Lanning Roper and His Gardens")

It was to be another four long years before I found my niche, one that was to allow me to use all my years of experience in one garden, whilst both gardening and using my design skills. I have never had so many good ideas day after day as when I work in the garden.

The early to mid-nineties saw the beginning of a great upsurge in gardening interest, generated primarily by the mass media of television and commercialism. Along with its benefits came the drawbacks, as all-and-sundry caught the "gravy train", claiming they were gardeners, or designers, with many gardens and their owners succumbing as it were to the "cowboys". So the professionals had to get more professional, and with the help of colleges and better television programmes, the industry has discarded much of the "chaff".

Of course, even in professionalism there is always room for criticism; as in most forms of art, it is down to personal taste. But the era had opened up the opportunity for all kinds of weird and wonderful ideas to be tried out, and if those "elements" and "principles" were not in place, then the end product would never sit comfortably, and would, I hope, not catch the eye of Val Roberts.

As I arrived at the manor in the late nineties, I

felt there was a need to introduce a more typically "English" flavour to the garden, which would stretch out to the less formal area at the top of the main lawn. This gave me the opportunity to introduce old roses as well as creating a "rose rope" along the existing terraces.

What every gardener needs is a cast iron back with a hinge on it.

Friday, 17th September, 2004 was a warm, damp, still, autumn day, though visibility was clear. As the daylight hours were drawing in, my thoughts turned to winter projects while I sat on a rock beside a small waterfall I had built that, due to a dry spell, was gently trickling into a pool, echoing its sound beneath a timber bridge before making its way downstream into the main pond. All this had been part of my landscaping project in an area of the garden that was knee-deep in mud, water and leaf mould when I arrived at the manor seven and a half years ago. Finally, after draining, cleaning ditches, diverting watercourses, bringing rocks from the woods to be strategically placed, planting, and erecting a seven-foot high deer fence, it had all settled back into its woodland environment.

The benefits of developing this top part of the garden had given interest, whilst allowing a more comfortable approach to the woods beyond.

However, the last two years had seen less interest in the garden from my employers. Continued development of major plans had come to a halt. Their time was taken up in many other areas, leaving me alone.

Having relished and enjoyed the many challenges the manor had presented over the years, I was now aware that my physical capabilities were not what they had been. With no walled or enclosed areas, it was very exposed and required a high maintenance programme. Bringing it back from neglect through to a manicured finish within the formal areas had been extremely satisfying, but major projects had been fraught with difficulties, and it would have been foolish of me to think that there would be any

The potting shed at the manor with some of the produce I grew for the house. The quiet of the potting shed during the winter months allowed me to make notes for my book.

more progress made.

The situation had now left me finding it difficult to retain any interest or enthusiasm for the continuing future plans I had. Although these were not on the scale of those that had passed, they would still require some input from my employers.

As any gardener will know, keeping the balance between man and nature requires an insatiable appetite to move forward. Therefore, it is imperative that we are constantly preparing the way, for not only plant regeneration, but also for the very facilities and conditions that allow that process to take place. That appetite to move forward is borne from the "elements", they will not let nature stand still, a garden does not stand still, it requires a process. A process that has the qualities of nurturing, of endurance and stamina, of patience; it is a labour of love. From that love are born fresh ideas, keeping the garden alive. Without that love, it will simply die.

On returning to work after the first part of my holidays, I had been given the go-ahead for a new greenhouse. This was indeed very welcome. It may be that life had taken an unexpected course for my employers in terms of family commitments, and indeed, their having to embrace change, but with my senior years now approaching, I knew that I must also think of my domestic situation and my health, being realistic about my physical capabilities towards retirement. Although the thought of having to leave the manor and my employers saddened me, I had to take comfort in the hope that my years of handiwork there would be of some benefit to whoever might follow in my footsteps, and hoped that they would be understanding enough to let me grow and move forward.

Conclusion

---

*"Gardening restores my inner peace, I am totally at peace
with myself in a garden. But no man is an island, and man
is involved in mankind."*

Wednesday, 3rd November, 2004. So, once again, has time
run its course? It is indeed a strange feeling as I begin this
conclusion. Like turning the cairn on one of my many fell
races, that feeling that you have done, done by reaching the
pinnacle, even though you have still got the home straight;
and that pinnacle is at different heights, with different pain
barriers for each of us. But let no man let it pass by. The
hurt in me is to overwhelm me with emotion as I rush my
pen forward with no less exhilaration than that which filled
me as I tumbled my way back from the fells to the finish
line; but this finish line has brought me through fifty years,
and terrain I could never have imagined.

Someone once said to me, *'You should never wonder why,'*
but never explained to me why: which, paradoxically, left
me wondering 'why'.

On the eve of the 29th December 1980, whilst driving
home after our evening meal, Helen asked me to pull in.
I was smitten with romance, and can vividly remember
the spot I chose. We began chatting, during which time I
detected some concern in her voice. Without pressing her,
she explained how happy she was about our engagement
but did not think I would want to go ahead and marry her
due to something in which she had been involved before
meeting me. Without going into detail, it left me feeling
that I just wanted to protect her, and I was so pleased she

had confided in me that it just brought us closer together. For me, there was no question of not going ahead with our marriage plans; but as I sit here and write, with no wife and no son, I do – "wonder why".

The timing is unreal, as I bring this book to a close almost exactly twelve years after I began. For the time span has been daunting, though not as daunting as the content, some of which so beguiled me in the beginning. In many ways, I feel that my hand has been guided whilst writing, knowing that throughout this time I could not have concluded, until now.

Whenever anyone has asked me how long I have been at any particular job, it has always raised a cause for concern within me, knowing my inability to stay anywhere for little longer than twelve months. This became a source of amusement to friends and family, as I would move on yet again to another experience. But, ironically, looking back, those experiences have come together as one job over the last twelve years – my book. The fact that I have now reached job number sixty-eight at the manor does not, in itself, suggest that I should be moving on. In fact, to the contrary, as I am so proud of my eight years here; but I remain a free spirit, and sensitive to change, which may be out of my control, and it is that which will prepare me for my next challenge, whether it is at the manor or elsewhere.

It has been an extraordinary existence over the past eight years, during which I have worked on the manor garden, renovated my house, completed writing my book, and spent many happy times with my son. This has led to a somewhat insular lifestyle, leaving me finding it difficult to talk about any particular current day subject except gardening.

"If you love a garden you will never be lonely, bored or idle, for you will always see beauty at the window: Autumn, Winter, Summer, Spring. Every changing season, its delight will bring."

I now feel ready to explore the outside world again, and hopefully make more garden visits. Though I may appear hapless to people who have had a more lucrative lifestyle, I retain a deep inner contentment that I value more than any wealth. This is a quality I feel has grown within me from childhood, probably due to mum and my grandparents reminding me to *'Make the most of what you've got.'*

People tend to size each other up according to what they possess. We consider folk with desirable cars, homes or lifestyles to be successful. We feel sorry for those who have less. True contentment though, stems from gratitude for the simple gift of life. With that you are rich beyond measure. Without it, there is no solace in spending power. If you seek the right priority, whatever else you need will come naturally.

"You take the crowded city street with life and shop galore;
I'll take the little woodland path down by the river shore,
You take the public garden, where all is arranged by plan;
I'll take the scenes laid out by God
And undisturbed by man.

You take the fountain on the lawn and listen to its tale;
I'll listen to the little brook that murmurs in the vale.
You live the artificial life and I will live the real;
And joy will come to me in mine
That yours can ne'er reveal."

(Extract from the book "A Springtime Saunter" by
Whiteley Turner)

It is that which is not tangible that can frighten us the most, causing us confusion and, in turn, making us take the easy way out by "pooh-poohing" something that we find difficult to believe in.

Acceptance of a greater force than mortal man has allowed me to enjoy life itself with more ease. Whilst seeing frustration and puzzlement on the faces of some at times when I may appear complex, this only serves to make me more determined to convey my message within this book – that it is the opposite, and although life continues to present us with more questions than answers, my belief and faith allow me to take a simple approach and be at ease with myself.

"The eyes are the windows of your soul."

With all the statistics in place for man's mortality rate, it signifies to me that my fifty years of existence have been allotted at least to allow me to write this book.

We must keep re-evaluating ourselves and our position at certain stages of our lives, so as not to lose sight of who we are, and our purpose in life. This surely helps us to move forward and enjoy life to the full.

As control is taken away from us at certain times and stages of our lives, we must recognise this, that our deed is done, and as a sign to move on. So please don't give up, but just continue with your next task.

It is important not to be obsessive, and whilst some of us have more of an addictive nature than others, these areas require much self-discipline. Life is a process of understanding human kind, and there is nothing gained worth having that does not bear some kind of sacrifice or pain. Remember, if you find a path with no obstacles, it probably doesn't lead anywhere. The burden of debt can result in losing sight of your ambition, and self-discipline is needed to keep steadily aiming towards your goal.

Instant success is usually short-lived, and things that come easily are rarely worth having. It is what you build slowly that passes the test of time and however slowly this building is done, it requires "action". It is natural for us all often to take a look at what has gone before, leaving us with a stark reminder that "action speaks louder than words", and what we do matters more than what we say.

I feel relieved that I have remained focused throughout my

writing without being consumed. I am not of an addictive nature, believing that balance is important in most things, but we "Yorkies" are known for keeping our feet firmly on the ground.

One of the most important qualities we can acquire in our childhood is "scruples". They are the foundation for us to strive to do what we think is good for ourselves and others. Once we reach independence, it is even more important to try and carry these through to our offspring.

Although adulthood teaches us the sciences and "grown-up" way of looking at the world, this can bring with it too much seriousness. We must be careful not to lose sight of certain values such as humour, and other simple ways of accepting and enjoying life, which were taught to us as children. I do hope that Dale will remember some of the niceties of his childhood to help keep his feet firmly on the ground should times ever get difficult for him as he grows.

My deepest love and thanks go to my son Dale, who has been unfortunate to witness some of his father's saddened times at such an early age, but who gave me such tender support and encouragement in the early years. So, Dale, should you ever think that I may, not only as a father but as a friend, be able to serve you in any way on life's journey, wherever I may be, this mortal man remains forever willing. May you know the quiet beauty of a walk in the country and keep it in your heart forever.

We are all aware of who has played a major role in our lives, though probably not always able to realise the influence and effect they have had on us. To this end, it is the reader who will have determined who has been my main influence, and inspiration, for writing this book.

A mum's constant concern for her children can, at times, become tiresome for both her and her brood yet, at the same time, remains no less than admirable. Mum instinctively knows whenever any one of us is a little low or finding things difficult. However hard we try to conceal these times, she will eventually find out in her way. One such time recently, due to my not seeing Dale for a long period, was in conversation on the telephone. Although she may not have realised, two words that mum said to me in such a quiet, pleading way were: *'don't weaken'*.

I have probably heard her and other people say these words many times, but there was something so meaningful in the way she delivered those words, I shall never forget. She believes in prayer, in herself, and lives for her children. It is, therefore, my deepest wish that you will know, mum, the unspoken love a son has for his mother, and that Dale too will let it be known on his part – "mum's the word".

The task of keeping this book a secret for so long has been enormous; especially with mum's instincts being so finely tuned. There have been times on the telephone when I feel sure that she has been suspicious about how I have been filling my time, but has never taken it upon herself to "dig deep", as I know she would have been capable of doing. This ongoing strain has been balanced by my being able to release in this form, page by page, the complicated route which my life has taken since I was born. Something has been locked up inside me for so long, and as each day, each month, each year passed, it became harder to find the end of the thread which would enable me to brief anyone on my past, should they show any interest. Ultimately, this left me embarrassed with a closed door. It has taken a lifetime to find the key – this book – which has allowed that thread to run through it page by page with the ease I could not have achieved verbally; but once that door was opened, it was something I just had to do.

Events that have occurred whilst writing have taken me beyond the expectations with which I set out, and have enabled me against all the odds to finish the book. Daily diaries have been essential in recording dates and places, along with conversations with mum, who unwittingly gave information. Aware that some parts may be sensitive reading, it has never been my intention to offend, and I hope that readers will understand my need to tell it as it was. I feel it is now my responsibility to ensure that mum is the first person to read my book, and hope that it will be received with careful understanding. For the many times in years gone by that something has prompted mum to exclaim, '*I could write a bloody book!*''- well, mum, I have written it for you.

For my son's sake, I hope that it will help to piece together parts of his life, and likewise, be received with careful understanding.

Mum's "young at heart" approach to life has helped her maintain contact with her children through the years, as well as enabling her to cope with all the stress which comes from raising a family. As she has watched us grow, I can only say how proud I am of her achievements of parenting, grand parenting, and great grand parenting, as just a few days ago, in her 75th year, her eldest son announced that she was a great grandma for the third time.

Her involvement with her family has quite often left little time and comfort for herself, so it comes as a pleasure, not soon enough, finally to see her enjoying some much deserved time and comfort. I hope that mum's restless years have been eased, and she may finally enjoy peace of mind.

Being able to see my life written down in front of me has somehow helped me to accept my own shortcomings as well as those of others. This has now left me feeling uncluttered, and with a refreshing feeling for life itself.

It remains now for me to thank everyone who has helped and encouraged me along the way in keeping contact with my son. Life can be taken away from us at less than a moment's notice. Just being with those you love is enough.

As for where my life carries on from here, I can only hope to embrace it as it continues to unfold. I am a tactile person, and living alone can be difficult at times, but there seems to be a danger in loving one person too much. Sometimes love doesn't seem to be enough, which makes me cautious about anyone being able to touch my heart again.

Whatever results from my completing this book, I am no greater and no lesser a man, but much the wiser.

> *"Trees are a symbol of stability in our ever-changing fragile world."*

A recent journey over to mum's took me past a site in Luddenden Foot where "British Furtex", the last working mill in the valley, had been demolished in this summer of 2004. It was indeed sad, knowing it was one of many that gave work to hundreds of local families (including mine) since the Industrial Revolution back in the 1800s. The vista it has opened up will create yet another change. Whether it be for alternative industry, planting or housing, it is just another section of life that hopefully will move forward, giving benefit to someone.

The adrenalin that now runs through me is for those who have read and reached this end, and who will move forward with their lives. If only by breaking one barrier, at least you will have crossed that threshold and my book will not have been in vain, but will have given you hope, as it has many times been given to me. So, however black those clouds may be, always – "look for the silver lining". (This day, Sunday, 7th November, 2004).

> *"I am not bound to succeed, but I am bound to live by the light that I am."*
>
> *"What's in a name? That which we call a rose by any other name would smell as sweet."*

William Shakespeare

When I Was Just A Lad

I often think back to the days when I was just a lad,
I wandered through the country lanes, past hillsides heather
  clad.
The sun was warm, the breeze a sigh, the streams in merry
  mood,
And little could be heard above a songbird and her brood.

The sights and sounds were a delight and in the tangled bushes,
Were busy little sparrows, with a singsong from the thrushes.
Those days of wide-eyed wonder, when I'd opened Nature's door,
And even viewed with pleasure, scenes I'd known before.

And changing brought new colour to familiar views,
Among the faithful sentinels: oaks, ashes, beeches, yews.
Days wandering in Yorkshire, all adventure and fun,
With warmth that spread through winter 'neath a hazy, watery
  sun.

A bite to eat atop a hill, while viewing Nature's bounty,
And glad to be a tiny part of our fine, green county.
Deciduous trees, wide and tall, and proud as was their right,
And in those days there never was a conifer in sight.

Such magic days of warmth and sun, adventure and endeavour,
Those days are gone, but in my heart, they'll be with me forever.
Such carefree days, all pleasure filled, their passing is so sad,
They sparkle in my memory, days when I was just a lad.

And I still view these pastures green, though changes I can see,
Yorkshire's fine, soft-curved hills look just as good to me.
And I appreciate these things, yes, everything I've had,
Not just today, but from way back to when I was just a lad.

(Anonymous)
